Old Man in an Old Car

Vernon Coleman

Books by Vernon Coleman include:

Medical
The Medicine Men
Paper Doctors
Everything You Want To Know About Ageing
The Home Pharmacy
Aspirin or Ambulance
Face Values
Stress and Your Stomach
A Guide to Child Health
Guilt
The Good Medicine Guide
An A to Z of Women's Problems
Bodypower
Bodysense
Taking Care of Your Skin
Life without Tranquillisers
High Blood Pressure
Diabetes
Arthritis
Eczema and Dermatitis
The Story of Medicine
Natural Pain Control
Mindpower
Addicts and Addictions
Dr Vernon Coleman's Guide to Alternative Medicine
Stress Management Techniques
Overcoming Stress
The Health Scandal
The 20 Minute Health Check
Sex for Everyone
Mind over Body
Eat Green Lose Weight
Why Doctors Do More Harm Than Good
The Drugs Myth

Complete Guide to Sex
How to Conquer Backache
How to Conquer Pain
Betrayal of Trust
Know Your Drugs
Food for Thought
The Traditional Home Doctor
Relief from IBS
The Parent's Handbook
Men in Bras, Panties and Dresses
Power over Cancer
How to Conquer Arthritis
How to Stop Your Doctor Killing You
Superbody
Stomach Problems – Relief at Last
How to Overcome Guilt
How to Live Longer
Coleman's Laws
Millions of Alzheimer Patients Have Been Misdiagnosed
Climbing Trees at 112
Is Your Health Written in the Stars?
The Kick-Ass A–Z for over 60s
Briefs Encounter
The Benzos Story
Dementia Myth

Psychology/Sociology
Stress Control
How to Overcome Toxic Stress
Know Yourself (1988)
Stress and Relaxation
People Watching
Spiritpower
Toxic Stress
I Hope Your Penis Shrivels Up
Oral Sex: Bad Taste and Hard To Swallow
Other People's Problems
The 100 Sexiest, Craziest, Most Outrageous Agony Column

Questions (and Answers) Of All Time
How to Relax and Overcome Stress
Too Sexy To Print
Psychiatry
Are You Living With a Psychopath?

Politics and General
England Our England
Rogue Nation
Confronting the Global Bully
Saving England
Why Everything Is Going To Get Worse Before It Gets Better
The Truth They Won't Tell You...About The EU
Living In a Fascist Country
How to Protect & Preserve Your Freedom, Identity & Privacy
Oil Apocalypse
Gordon is a Moron
The OFPIS File
What Happens Next?
Bloodless Revolution
2020
Stuffed
The Shocking History of the EU
Coming Apocalypse
Covid-19: The Greatest Hoax in History
Old Man in a Chair
Endgame
Proof that Masks do more harm than Good
Covid-19: The Fraud Continues
Covid-19: Exposing the Lies
Social Credit: Nightmare on Your Street
NHS: What's wrong and how to put it right
They want your money and your life.
Their Terrifying Plan

Diaries and Autobiographies
Diary of a Disgruntled Man
Just another Bloody Year

Bugger off and Leave Me Alone
Return of the Disgruntled Man
Life on the Edge
The Game's Afoot
Tickety Tonk
Memories 1
Memories 2
Memories 3
My Favourite Books
Truth Teller: The Price

Animals
Why Animal Experiments Must Stop
Fighting For Animals
Alice and Other Friends
Animal Rights – Human Wrongs
Animal Experiments – Simple Truths

General Non Fiction
How to Publish Your Own Book
How to Make Money While Watching TV
Strange but True
Daily Inspirations
Why Is Public Hair Curly
People Push Bottles Up Peaceniks
Secrets of Paris
Moneypower
101 Things I Have Learned
100 Greatest Englishmen and Englishwomen
Cheese Rolling, Shin Kicking and Ugly Tattoos
One Thing after Another
Vernon Coleman's Dictionary of Old English Words and Phrases

Novels (General)
Mrs Caldicot's Cabbage War
Mrs Caldicot's Knickerbocker Glory
Mrs Caldicot's Oyster Parade
Mrs Caldicot's Turkish Delight

Deadline
Second Chance
Tunnel
Mr Henry Mulligan
The Truth Kills
Revolt
My Secret Years with Elvis
Balancing the Books
Doctor in Paris
Stories with a Twist in the Tale (short stories)
Dr Bullock's Annals
The Awakening of Dr Amelia Leighton
A Needle for a Needle (novella)

The Young Country Doctor Series
Bilbury Chronicles
Bilbury Grange
Bilbury Revels
Bilbury Country
Bilbury Village
Bilbury Pie (short stories)
Bilbury Pudding (short stories)
Bilbury Tonic
Bilbury Relish
Bilbury Mixture
Bilbury Delights
Bilbury Joys
Bilbury Tales
Bilbury Days
Bilbury Memories

Novels (Sport)
Thomas Winsden's Cricketing Almanack
Diary of a Cricket Lover
The Village Cricket Tour
The Man Who Inherited a Golf Course
Around the Wicket
Too Many Clubs and Not Enough Balls

Cat books
Alice's Diary
Alice's Adventures
We Love Cats
Cats Own Annual
The Secret Lives of Cats
Cat Basket
The Cataholics' Handbook
Cat Fables
Cat Tales
Catoons from Catland

As Edward Vernon
Practice Makes Perfect
Practise What You Preach
Getting Into Practice
Aphrodisiacs – An Owner's Manual
The Complete Guide to Life

Play
Mrs Caldicot's Cabbage War

Written with Donna Antoinette Coleman
How to Conquer Health Problems between Ages 50 & 120
Health Secrets Doctors Share With Their Families
Animal Miscellany
England's Glory
Wisdom of Animals

Copyright Vernon Coleman May 2024
The right of Vernon Coleman to be identified as the author of this work has been asserted in accordance with the Copyright, Designs and Patents Act 1988.

Dedication

To Antoinette, the love of my life and beyond: you are my hope, my purpose, my inspiration, my reason. You are all my delights, all my joys, all my hopes, all my ambitions, all my happiness. Thank you for being you and for being with me.

Preface

This began as a book about buying an old car as one last absurd adventure. But I realised that the old car was a perfect analogy not just for what happens to us and how we change as we get older, but also how we should, perhaps, respond to those changes.

So, for example, the car's clock and the petrol gauge don't work. Should I get them investigated, diagnosed and repaired (at enormous expense) or should I put up with the faults? If I take the car to the garage (and only a specialist garage can look after old, classic cars) it will be away and out of use for weeks on end.

I'm a little deaf and losing my hair and I get out of breath if I walk up steep hills. I also wobble more than I'd like. Should I see endless doctors, have tests and investigations done and take tablets which probably cause the A to Z of side effects? Or should I just put up with these annoyances, and regard them as just a part of growing old? (I see people who are ten years older than I am running marathons and I am in awe. How did they age so well? Did they live on lentils and pastoral evocations?)

Looking at an old car confirms that progress often isn't progress at all, though we are told it always is. Are electric windows necessarily better than windows you wind up and down? The former go wrong more often than the latter. How much effort does it take to operate a window winder? When a windscreen wiper blade needs replacing, is it better to replace just the blade or the whole wiper mechanism?

Are modern cars too complicated for their own (and our) good? Is the progress we are told we must applaud, always 'progress'?

And so this book about an old car changed course and somehow it became a philosophy book, a commonplace book, a book about things it took me a lifetime to learn, and a book which contains as much (or more) about the reflections of an old man, and about how our world has changed, as about the old car. It is a book of observations and memories; it is a book about the myriad ways in which the world has changed (mainly or exclusively for the worst I'm afraid) and is now virtually unrecognisable. Comparing today's world with the world a few decades ago is like comparing a seven course meal at Maxims with a packet of Hula Hoops. It's all food but they're very different. (I should, perhaps, explain, en passant, that a commonplace book, popular in the 19th century, was a volume in which were collected thoughts, sayings and anecdotes which the author thought worth saving and sharing.)

The world seems different when you get older and that's just because it is different. It was ever thus. Everything changes.

But it's different this time.

It's different because everything is changing far more speedily than ever before.

But it's also different because everything old is now dismissed as clapped out and useless. And that means people as much as 20th century mobile phones.

Other civilisations may have revered their elderly, and learnt from them, but our civilisation regards elderly machinery as fit only for the scrapyard and elderly people as suitable candidates for euthanasia. Do not resuscitate. Do not pass Go. Do not collect £200.

This isn't a book full of nostalgia and sentimental reflections studied through the flattering lens of time and the deceptively reassuring retrospectoscope. It's a look at what we've lost, what we ended up with and where we're going now – in a world dominated and controlled by distant rentiers who regard megalomania as a virtue not a sin. And it is an exploration of the ageing processes which bewilder and astound everyone who lives long enough to discover the mental and physical cost of getting old. And it's about an old car.

When writing fiction I've often found that the characters decide what is going to happen to them, and just take me along for the ride. That may be a cliché but clichés are clichés because they're often true. So, for example my novel 'Mrs Caldicot's Cabbage War' was a very different book when I first sat down to write it. My intention was that Mrs Caldicot and her chums would rob a bank. (The idea was original then.) But Mrs Caldicot took over and made it clear that she didn't want to rob a bank. And so the book (and the subsequent movie) took a different direction.

The same thing happened to me as I wrote this book.

Authors and publishers are required to categorise their books. But I have no idea how this book should be filed. Is it an autobiography?

Is it a book of philosophy? Is it a book of essays or humorous pieces? An old-fashioned and rushed book shop assistant would probably put it on the shelf headed 'Motor Car Maintenance'. Maybe it should be filed under 'Rambling'. Or would that merely result in a lot of walkers being disappointed?

I can, however, tell you this.

In 1782 and 1789, the two parts of Jean-Jacques Rousseau's book 'Les Confessions' were published and are now widely recognised as the first modern autobiography. (Rousseau died in 1778, of course. His book was published posthumously and the two parts were later combined as one.)

The book begins: 'This is what I have done and this is what has been done to me. If on occasions I have added some innocent embellishment, it has been only to fill the odd defect of character. Sometimes I may have taken for a fact what was no more than a probability, but I have never put down what I knew to be false.'

I stand with M. Rousseau on this.

Vernon Coleman, Bilbury, Devon
May 2024

It arrived, in some state, in the back of a specialist, covered low loader brought, safe and dry, from the auction house. The driver of the low loader lowered the ramp at the back, opened the doors, unfastened a variety of safety straps, and reversed the vehicle, which was inside the low loader, down the ramp and onto the road. It was the first time we'd seen it. I climbed in and reversed the car through our gates and into a parking space on our driveway where it would not be in the way but could be picked up by another low loader and taken to a specialist garage for a service. The car had not been used for quite a while and we knew it would need some attention to make sure that it was safe to drive.

When the driver of the low loader had gone, we climbed back into the car and shut the doors. We didn't start the engine or do anything other than just sit there. Old cars have a unique atmosphere of their own and standing beside or sitting inside a 1957 Bentley S type is to find joy in a crooked, grubby world.

The Bentley S was the last four-seater sports saloon of note and it is a car which could comfortably stand in a museum as a work of art. The standard model cost £4,669.00 and it was the last beautiful car made before designers were encouraged (and later forced) to produce cars which obeyed standard aerodynamic regulations and, as a result, all looked the same. It was the last car built at a time when small boys were proud to be able to identify most of the cars on the road simply by the silhouette. It was built when speed, good looks and comfort were the ultimate criteria.

Just as city planners have steadily, deliberately and with quiet determination destroyed the world's urban conurbations by demolishing every old and handsome building and replacing them with tributes to the temporary and uncomfortable joys of concrete and glass, so bureaucrats have permanently destroyed the joy of looking at, owning and driving motor cars.

The S type was the first Bentley built for the owner to drive, rather than being built to be driven by a chauffeur in a uniform and a peaked hat. Many earlier cars provided a box for the passengers and left the driver sitting outside, unprotected, just as the drivers of horse driven vehicles had sat out in the rain and the snow and the hot sun.

That philosophy ended forever in the 1950s, and it ended with the Bentley S type and its twin the Rolls Royce Silver Cloud. (The two cars are pretty much identical other than their very individual hood ornaments.)

The Bentley S type was the last car built with a proper chassis, hand-crafted by proud men who spent their lives making the best motor vehicles that could be made and who, when they retired, did so with massive pride in their life's work. It was by no means uncommon for a craftsman who had spent his life building Bentleys to retire, spend his life's savings on an old Bentley and then spend his retirement years restoring it. Other retirees supplemented their pensions by doing servicing and restoration work for the owners of these cars. And they often did it as much for the joy of what they were doing than for any decent financial reward.

The S type Bentley (later to be known as the Bentley S1 when the company produced an S2 version and then an S3 version is a glorious symbol of simpler, better days. It was produced in a time when even mass produced, relatively cheap vehicles such as the Morris Minor were solidly made – so solidly made that you can still see a few of them on the roads, being used as every day vehicles. The S type is a motor car symbolic of quality, respect, value and dignity; a car big enough to fit the Royal Philharmonic Orchestra in the back with their instruments packed neatly in the boot. Together with its twin, the Rolls Royce Silver Cloud, the Bentley S1 is one of the most iconic British motor cars and stands together with the Silver Ghost, the Mini and the Aston Martin DB5 as the finest examples of motor car manufacture.

William Morris wisely said that we should own only those things which are practical or useful. When, oh when, did we decide to ignore that good advice? If William Morris came back and bought a motor car he would buy a Bentley S type.

Even the owner's manual for the car is beautifully made. It is (of course) a hardback book and it is fastened with a press stud so that things don't get pushed between the pages when the manual is stored in the glove compartment. And the manual doesn't just look good, it is also the most sensible and simply written document of its kind I've ever seen, with none of the ambiguities, omissions, misspellings and errors which are the collective hallmark of modern manuals. (The solitary exception was the manual for the first printer I ever bought. It was made, I remember, by Hewlett Packard and the instructions began with the words: 'Place the printer's plug in a convenient wall socket'.

Bentley only made just over 3,000 of these cars for world-wide distribution, with some having left hand drive and a few more were built with slightly different bodies, and I can't help wondering how many are left. No one seems to know how many exist though a sensible guess is that, spread around the world, there are probably around 1,000 left. Other cars, made by the million, are probably rarer. The Bentleys survived not because they were more expensive but because they were better made and more loved than almost all other cars.

We had decided that it would be a delight to try to save one. And we bought it at auction, sight unseen.

I looked at the car we'd bought and realised that although it was an entirely pointless purchase it was also absolutely necessary. And it will, I know, keep us in touch with part of our history and culture that the globalists are determined to eradicate.

Spending £15,000 (plus the auctioneer's commission) to buy a car unseen probably sounds reckless but I had seen a short film of the car being driven and I'd seen a huge portfolio of photographs of the car – including pictures of the outside, the inside, the engine compartment and even the underneath of the car. I'd certainly seen as much of the car as I would have seen if I'd spent two days travelling to look at it.

Buying the Bentley was probably reckless and definitely not the sort of thing a bank manager would countenance.

We obviously don't need a 67-year-old car. We have vehicles which can and do provide us with all the transport we need.

For me, it was my last hoorah; my last quiet and dignified farewell salute to a world in which expediency and superficiality have overtaken respect and dignity; a world in which the word 'disposable' now seems to apply to houses and motor cars as much as it once applied to paper picnic plates and cheap, leaky, plastic ballpoint pens. I very much wanted to share this special joy with Antoinette, my wife.

Legislation introduced and approved at the behest of commercial lobbyists means that most people live in houses which are put together with the ceilings too low and the walls too close together.

The people who have put themselves in charge have given us a miserable world in which walls are made of such thin material that noise and cold travel through without difficulty. They've given us houses which have such small rooms that there are no built-in cupboards, larders or pantries. The ultimate lunacy is that the bureaucrats have for decades been forcing people to knock down Victorian houses on the dubious and largely meaningless grounds that the doorways aren't wide enough. They've been replacing solid, warm houses which have lasted well over a century, and which are well enough built to last at least another century, with cardboard boxes which will almost certainly fall down within two decades.

The same brand of cut price idiots have overseen the design and building of cars which all look the same, which crumple in a breeze and which are absurdly over complicated, packed with unnecessary and confusing safety features.

The S type may be old, and patently from another time, but it is a work of art. It deserves to be looked after, loved and, most of all, to be used. It has a right to survive. It provides a special cultural link with our past; a link which connects us to better times.

We live in a disposable age. Everything else you can think of is made according to fashion and economy rather than anything else. Everything is designed to have a remarkably short life. When I was young I had a bicycle which lasted several decades of tough, daily riding. When the frame eventually broke I got through two replacements in five years. Electrical equipment may be cheaper than it used to be, but it is also less sturdy, less reliable and more difficult to use.

We live in the age of the temporary and the disposable.

Most authors know (and I am no exception in this regard) that their work will be dead and forgotten within a decade or two at most. When our last existing reader dies or loses interest then our books will quietly disappear. Publishers used to take care of their back lists and even dead authors received some care. Today, publishers want authors who appear regularly on television, who are invited onto reality TV programmes and who have active social media accounts. Authors over the age of 60 are already close to being forgotten. Only a very tiny percentage of books and authors are likely to be remembered. The same thing goes for music, films, and art. This is the age of the gimmick. The constant question is: 'What's next?'

Most vehicles have only a transient life, of course. However much they appeal to their individual fan groups the majority of cars will, within a few decades of their launch, be remembered only in old photographs and books. And then the photographs and books will disappear too. And when the last drivers to have owned, enjoyed and taken pride in a Ford Consul or Hillman Imp die or forget their pride and joy then the model will disappear.

I believe that the Bentley S type is, and deserves to be, a different sort of creation. It represents a level of craftsmanship and design that will almost certainly never be seen again. It is rare, beautiful and part of our nation's history. In most countries, old buildings are listed and protected, though it must be said that in the UK the listing system seems to have become a battleground between the preservationists who want to protect old houses and the climate change enthusiasts who want to demolish any house with a chimney and casement windows and to disfigure old houses by fitting them with heat pumps and plastic framed, triple glazed windows. Old cars with style should also be protected.

We all have red letter days in our lives.

My two leading Red Letter Days are the one when I met my wife and the day when we got married. But there are minor Red Letter Days too, of course, and the day our Bentley was delivered is definitely well-established on that list.

Our new old car is blue, Lugano Blue since you are kind enough to ask, with a thin hand-painted coach stripe in red. It is a beautiful and rare colour. It is probably the only blue S1 left in England. It may well be the only blue S1 in the world. Most of the Bentley S cars seem to be black or beige. The car sparkles in the sunshine and apart from a few patches of rust on the chrome, it is close to perfect. Inside, the soft, leather upholstery is red and as battered and wrinkled as you might expect it to be. There are, I confess, a couple of tears in the leather. We don't much care though we will maybe have the front bench seat reupholstered.

As I've already noted, the car has so far cost us £15,000 plus another £2,250 for the auctioneer's premium and a fee of £1,000 for the low loader to bring the car a couple of hundred miles from the auction house. Under £20,000 is not far north of the sort of price usually paid for an old Bentley car which is about to be broken up and used for spares. The auctioneer's estimate was £8,000 to £12,000 but auctioneer's estimates are always low.

Nothing from an old Bentley is ever wasted. Those cars which are too battered and broken down to save (and it's repairing the body work rather than the engine which costs the big money) are carefully disarticulated so that the parts can be sold. There's a continuous demand for spares and nothing is wasted. Bits of bodywork, bits of engine, electrical parts and so on are all put on sale, and often carry quite high prices. No one is mass producing spare parts for 67-year-old cars, and anything which cannot be reclaimed from an old car has to be specially made, or adapted from some other vehicle. The people who restore cars to show want to make sure that every part, however, minor is original and although we don't intend ever to show our car, we want to keep it honest. Putting wing mirrors from a Ford Mondeo onto an old Bentley would be uncomfortably close to sacrilegious.

But this Bentley isn't going to be broken up for spares. This car is starting a new life. And there are things which need attention.

The brakes on S type Bentleys are renowned for being terrible at slow, manoeuvring speeds but at the moment the brakes are well north of terrible and lie somewhere between terrifying and a blood curdling scream of anguish. At slow speeds I found that I could really only control the car by judicious use of the handbrake.

The second immediate problem is that although the car did start when we'd taken it out of the transporter, it doesn't start now. There is a problem with the ignition. I put the key into the ignition but it won't turn and there is obviously something wrong with the ignition box.

It's going to cost money. There are going to be moments of frustration and disappointment.

But I really, really don't care.

Meanwhile, just sitting in the car is a joy. The unique smell of wood and leather and decades of oil is wonderful. Any perfumier who could produce this smell in an atomiser and then sell it to modern car manufacturers would make a fortune.

In 2019 my beloved wife, Antoinette, was diagnosed with breast cancer. She had surgery and a month of radiotherapy and has been taking tamoxifen every day since then. She's also changed her diet and has dramatically cut down her intake of dairy produce (milk, butter and cheese). She has a hormone dependent form of the cancer, and there is a widely accepted belief that the hormones found in dairy foods are potentially dangerous. She has done everything she possibly can to keep the cancer at bay but, like thousands of people in the same situation, we both worry every day that a headache or a pain here or there could be a harbinger of something serious. The fear is never far away and provides us with an uncomfortable level of background anxiety. If your family has been touched by cancer (maybe the word 'molested by cancer' would be more appropriate) you will know what I mean when I say that the terror is always there; hiding behind every symptom, an unending, ever-present tyranny of quiet fears.

And then in the first half of 2023, we went through a dull, irritating, frustrating, boring six months. It was a half year full of some trivial and some costly annoyances. Our drains were blocked with tree roots and took four men around six days to unblock them. An upstairs radiator leaked and then, after the leaky radiator had been removed, the central heating boiler stopped and took several harsh winter months to get repaired. A beautiful silver birch suddenly died and had to be taken down. Inevitably, the tree surgeons we hired left us with huge tree trunk rounds, far too big for our fireplace, even though we had paid them to chop the tree into logs. The door to our lovely new greenhouse became stuck fast because the manufacturers had used unseasoned, unprotected wood which had warped in the wet weather. We found (by accident) that our website provider has for years been charging us twice for every one of the many services it seems necessary for it provide. They reimbursed some of the stolen money but there was, of course, no apology or explanation. We discovered wet rot in several joists, a window frame and a door and the roof developed five separate leaks. A bath tap came loose and fell off. The oven, the freezer and the dishwasher all stopped working in the space of ten days. The dishwasher could be mended. In a misguided effort to support local workmen, we used a local company to replace the oven and they rewarded our loyalty by charging us slightly more than twice the price which a better model might have cost us online – delivered and fitted. My laptop decided that it had worked hard enough and needed to go into a retirement home. And the condition must have been infectious because within a week Antoinette's laptop came to the same conclusion. Just to compound the problems, the letters R and C came off the keyboard of a spare laptop we found and refused to be glued back into position. A building society account decided that it was an amoeba, split itself into two for absolutely no reason and caused chaos. Our router acquired a mind of its own and our Wi-Fi disappeared. Our plug-in telephones stopped charging and then stopped working. Our sole television and DVD player both started playing up and refused to respond to instructions given by the hand held device. Everything in the house that was controlled by a remote device stopped working.

Attempts to ease the chaos caused more problems. Our bank started to play bandits and robbers and refused to let me access my own money. And a malignant mole, working for one of the deceitful agencies tasked with oppressing and silencing truth-tellers, quietly took control of one of my websites (www.vernoncoleman.org) and left us with no option but to close the site completely.

All that in just a few months that seemed to be interminable.

I found that I was constantly being harassed and cheated. We were scammed by an insurance company, the police sent us a threatening letter by mistake and a car park company stole money from us. And, naturally, the seemingly endless stream of workmen who made their way to our door all had ideas for putting as much of our money into their pockets as possible while doing as little as possible to earn it.

Oh and a long stretch of cast iron guttering crashed to the ground, smashing a wooden bench, causing considerable chaos and missing my head by thirty minutes or so. We managed to find a roofer who agreed to do the necessary repairs. He then went online (why do people do that?) found out that I am officially described as a 'discredited conspiracy theorist' and refused to do the work. The collapse of the ironwork drew attention to the fact that our Victorian home is rather in need of a good deal of repair work. Part of the problem is that for three years we've been rather too busy to organise essential painting and repair work.

The result was that we spent most of our time dealing with what can, most accurately, be described as crap – the sort of debilitating, garbage that disrupts and gradually saps the strength of mind and body. Other than Antoinette's illness, none of the things that happened was devastating but individually they were irritating and collectively they were dispiriting and boring. It's the drip, drip, drip that wears the hole in the stone.

And all this lay on top of an unceasing, damaging and unrewarding battle against the lies of the fraud which had marred the months and years after February 2020. I had already been banned from everywhere for the heinous modern crime of telling the truth. Publishers and agents who handled my books in 26 languages all decided I was too controversial and too hot to handle. Publishers who had previously been keen to print extracts from my books suddenly lost all interest. Newspaper editors and TV producers all stopped replying to emails and didn't return phone calls. I was permanently banned from all social media. YouTube even banned me from looking at other people's videos. And the Royal Society of Arts expelled me because one or two other fellows were upset at my telling inconvenient truths. (You'll find the whole extraordinary saga described in my book 'TruthTeller: The Price'.)

It's perhaps not surprising that we mislaid our joie de vivre.

Things started to get me down a little. Every time the postman came it was to bring more trouble. Every time I received an email it was bad news. Every time the telephone rang I flinched. It got to the point where I wanted to stay in bed for a month. Or find a pile of good books, light a log fire, ignore the world and sit down to read myself back to sanity.

I mention all this not to gain sympathy but merely to explain our state of mind when we decided we needed an adventure; we needed to put a little fun in our lives. If you don't do it yourself, no one else will do it for you.

For an hour or two we thought about taking a holiday.

It's nearly five years since we last stayed away from home for a night. We went to Yorkshire for a few days and although parts of it were excellent, it turned out to be something of a curate's egg. Every road we drove on (including the motorways) was seriously disrupted with road works (the usual kind – loads of cones and speed cameras but no one working), all the useful road signs had been removed (presumably in case the Germans invaded again) and there were speed cameras every few hundred yards (mostly hidden behind tree trunks and road furniture). We had booked an extremely expensive hotel for a treat and it was freezing cold. The receptionist told us that they had reduced the temperature in the hotel to protect the environment. She didn't mention that the hotel was saving money by keeping the rooms chilly. The water that came out of the hot tap was tepid at best and the excuse this time was that the hotel was obeying laws restricting the temperature of their boiler. The bedroom was grubby and the food inedible and served without grace or style.

We thought about a trip abroad but abandoned that thought very speedily. Travel by train or aeroplane has been made pretty well unbearable by absurd customs regulations and unpredictable strikes.

We aren't into the sort of luxuries which most people favour. We neither of us spend much money on clothes or shoes or on hairdressers. We never go to restaurants, the theatre or even the cinema. I spend more money than most people on books and DVDs but that's for my work and doesn't really count.

We thought, for a while, about finding a castle to renovate (they give them away with packets of porridge in Scotland) or a small farm to run. But we really couldn't face all the paperwork (endless discussions with estate agents, planning people, lawyers, bankers and so on) and we like where we live. So we quickly abandoned that notion.

We decided that we were homesick for another era and so we decided, possibly counter intuitively, that we would double down on the aggravation by buying something that would definitely be a lot of trouble but which wouldn't matter terribly whenever it broke down (i.e. not cause the sort of inconvenience and disruption which a broken freezer or oven can cause) but which would offer us a little old-fashioned fun.

So, with Antoinette's support, I did something quite deliberately reckless, defiant, pointless, anti-woke and, not to pussy foot around, undeniably stupid.

I felt I had one last silliness in me; one last hoorah.

And so I decided to buy an old, classic car.

Once you start looking at old cars it is clear that there is a huge choice available. There are many famous brand names that have either disappeared completely or been swallowed up by huge manufacturers. Back in the day when motorists wore goggles and motoring was an adventure there were some wonderful cars around.

We found a five seater Cubitt motor car, available in blue and fitted with an adjustable windscreen and a reverse gear as well as four forward gears. Early motorists looked upon a reverse gear as something of a luxury. But the Cubitt looked to be just too much trouble. Vauxhall, Singer and Humber made huge, solid, wonderful looking motor cars, and buyers looking for something exotic could purchase a Hispano-Suiza. Many of these old cars had absolutely huge engines, ten times the size of the engines fitted in modern family cars.

But, within minutes of making the decision to buy an old motor car, I had abandoned all other temptations and had decided to buy a 1957, S type Bentley sports saloon; a car which many car enthusiasts (and all Bentley aficionados) reckon was the last really great and beautiful car; it was, indeed, surely the last great artefact.

We hunted around through the car magazines and all the relevant internet sites. A couple of times we thought we'd found the right car for us. But we hadn't. On one occasion I offered to buy a Bentley S type from a dealer. We agreed a price of £32,000, which included delivery, and then he suddenly went quiet and I never heard anything else from him. I have no idea what happened to him. Maybe he looked me up on the internet and found that according to Google, global purveyor of universal lies, I am a 'discredited conspiracy theorist'. Who knows.

But the car was black and afterwards we were both pleased that we hadn't bought it. We'd have felt that we were either driving in the mayoral limousine or taking part in a funeral procession.

On another occasion we were about to agree a purchase when I noticed a dodgy looking area on one of the photographs we'd been sent. (We hadn't actually seen either of these cars. I know enough about cars to know that even an expert can't really tell whether a car is a good buy or not. You have to own it for a month before you know.) I asked to see more photos and from the second set it was clear that the paint had bubbled and was peeling. One of the most expensive problems to put right on an old car is the paintwork. Thirty odd years ago I had a Bentley T type in British racing green which was scratched along one side with a key while parked outside a police station. Attempts to deal with the scratches proved fruitless because the garage couldn't match the paint. Eventually I commissioned a complete bare metal re-spray which cost over £10,000. (The Bentley T type was a terrible buy. After I'd bought the car I discovered that the floor of the car was so rotten and full of holes that I could see the road underneath me as I drove along.)

And I have enough experience of car dealers to know that even those selling Bentleys and Rolls Royce motor cars are not above deceiving their customers. I once bought a Silver Cloud I from a very reputable dealer who assured me that the car had received a bare metal re-spray. This was exposed as a lie when a blister developed in the paint and it was clear that there were two paint colours visible underneath the black paint. The dealer had merely sprayed new paint on top of the previous coats of paint.

So, then I doubled down on the stupidity: I decided to buy a car at auction.

I've always liked auctions.

We have, over the years, bought a good deal of our furniture and many of the pictures on our walls from auctions. When we had an apartment in Paris we furnished it almost entirely with stuff we bought from a Depot Vente just a couple of hundred yards away from our apartment. (A Depot Vente isn't actually an auction house but it is remarkably similar. People take along stuff they want to sell and buyers can buy or make an offer. If you buy it you can take it home with you and, when the lift turns out to be too small, drag it up six flights of stairs if your apartment happens to be on the top floor.)

Around twenty years ago, we used to buy boxfuls of books from auction houses which specialised in rare books. In those days it was possible to buy assorted first editions for absurdly low prices. We would put low bids on a number of lots that we were interested in and then wait to see which lots we won. We used a carrier to pack the books, put them into crates and have them delivered to us. And then we had the fun of opening the crates, un-wrapping the books (which were all individually wrapped in thick brown paper as though they were rare Shakespearean folios) and examining our purchases. The book buying fun stopped when the auction houses which we used were taken over and became international. Two things happened. First the commission we had to pay rose massively (this, of course, was in addition to a similar commission which the seller had to pay). Second, we found that whenever we won a lot we always had to pay our top bid. If we had said that we would pay up to £200 for a lot then we would pay £200 (plus commission and transport). In addition, the American buyers, bidding over the internet, were paying higher prices than we thought reasonable. There were no bargains anymore and the fun went out of it.

Still, auctions can be interesting and, if you are both careful and lucky, a good way to buy something that you either need or just want. And, especially if you're bidding against dealers, you can always fool yourself that you've acquired a bargain.

We didn't need an old car but we wanted one and we weren't having a lot of luck buying through dealers or private sellers. Besides, we thought we'd have one thing in favour: American buyers weren't likely to be bidding on fairly lowly priced classic cars. The cost of shipping a car across the Atlantic is pretty steep. Add on the cost of insurance and the cost of transporting the car to the port, and the price becomes prohibitive.

And so I bid on an old car which was being sold at an auction several hundred miles away.

Although the previous owner had apparently been an elected official with the Bentley Drivers' Club, I knew the car would need work to make it roadworthy (though really old cars have the advantage of not needing to pass an MOT test) and if our bid was successful I decided that we'd do a rolling restoration. We'd have the car made safe and roadworthy and then drive it for a while, have some more work done on it, drive it for a while and so on. We knew that the downside risk was limited because old classic, collectible cars always have a value even when they're derelict. There is such a demand for the parts that a car of this type will always have a bottom line break-up value of £8,000 to £10,000.

I put a bid of £15,000 on the car, though that came with a hefty commission for the auctioneer on top. We knew that we'd have to spend about the same amount to make the car roadworthy, and we could have bought a restored but still imperfect car of the same age for between £30,000 and £40,000, but it seemed more sensible to do the restoration ourselves (or, rather, to pay a garage to do it). If we paid for our own restoration we'd know exactly what was being done.

I didn't go to the auction and I didn't even go and look at the car beforehand. I did read through the particulars on the auctioneer's website, and I looked at the lovely photographs they'd taken, but all I know about cars is that the good ones have an engine, a gear box, some brakes, a wheel at each corner and a wheel for the driver to sit behind. You probably think I'm kidding but I'm not. I've owned dozens of cars, some expensive, top of the range vehicles and, when I was a student, some broken down wrecks that would have been written off if anyone had ever tried to get them through a roadworthiness test (my first car, a huge Humber, cost £30) and a good number of them I've owned and driven without ever once looking underneath the bonnet. On several occasions, a breakdown mechanic has asked me to open the bonnet and I've had to find the manual and search through it to find out how to do it.

So looking at the car, crawling underneath and checking the engine compartment would have told me nothing. I had bought Bentleys in the past and although I had examined them carefully, both were disastrous purchases. It's just too easy to hide faults and problems. I had hired experts to check the cars but they were either incompetent or crooked because despite their assurances, the cars were disappointing and in nowhere as good condition as I was assured they were. (Despite the disappointment, I suffered from seller's remorse for many years after selling my other Bentley S.)

A number of books about Bentleys contain good advice on what to look for when buying an old Bentley – with comprehensive check lists to be carefully followed.

We didn't bother with any of that. We just put on a bid.

And rather to our delight, our bid won.

I have no idea how many other bidders there were or if they were indeed any other bidders. By one of those strange coincidences which are part of my life, the hammer price was my top bid. I find it surprising how often this happens.

I can imagine that there will be some who will question our sanity in paying out £15,000 for a 67-year-old car which we hadn't even seen.

But look at the sums.

If the Bentley has to be sold for scrap (heaven forbid) it could fetch around £12,000 to £15,000. In a year or two it will fetch more than that.

If we had bought a medium range family saloon costing, say £50,000, the car would lose around half of its value within two to three years.

So, from a purely financial point of view, the Bentley was a better buy.

And it looks better and is a darned sight more fun.

That's my rationale and it's got me convinced.

After the car arrived we sat in it for a while, admiring the workmanship. I have always admired well made things and I long ago realised that good, expensive things last much longer, in apparent good condition, than cheaper products. I have an Austin Reed sports coat which I bought in Regent Street in my 20s which is still perfectly serviceable (though the pockets are baggy from being stuffed with books and notebooks) and a Burberry trench coat which I bought in the 1990s and which looks as good as new. I have an old piece of canvas luggage which, judging by its present condition, will last at least another 200 years and will, as it acquires a patina of age, look even more respectable than it does at the moment. Mont Blanc pens and Swiss Army Penknives which I have had for years satisfy both of William Morris's requirements: they are beautiful and useful.

These days stuff is made to fall apart after it's been used once

And manufacturers find clever ways to wriggle out of any responsibility.

So, for example, when our boiler broke down, the engineer decided that the problem was a leak in the heat exchanger. The leak had caused the boiler to work intermittently and it had also damaged the electrics inside the boiler.

'Can we not claim on the warranty? I asked, when I was told the price of a new component.

'No, I'm afraid not,' was the reply. 'Not unless you've put more inhibitor into the system.'

'Why should I have put in more inhibitor?' I asked, naively.

'Because the system has been losing water because of the leak. And the system is supposed to contain the requisite quantity of inhibitor in order to satisfy the requirements of the warranty.'

'But it was the failure of the boiler which led to the leak?'

'Indeed, it was.'

'And there was no way that I could know that the system needed more inhibitor.'

'That's absolutely true.'

Since the boiler had pretty well destroyed itself because of the manufacturing fault we had to replace it and buy a new one, even though the faulty boiler was still within its warranty period.

Apparently boilers aren't made to last much longer than this anyway.

Much the same happens whenever anything goes wrong these days.

Our oven stopped working (and started producing vast quantities of toxic throat and chest burning smoke). The engineer we called took one look at it and told us that something had gone wrong. We thanked him for this observation and asked him if he could repair it. He spent around three minutes looking at it and then said we would need a new oven but that we were in luck because a local dealer with whom he had a 'relationship' could provide us with what we needed.

In the same week, an almost new chest freezer stopped freezing. After throwing away a large quantity of food that should have been frozen but wasn't, we found the guarantee and called the manufacturer. They sent a man who looked at the freezer and concluded that there was something wrong with it. (He was presumably trained at the same college as the man who spotted that our oven was faulty.) He had a bag of tools and, after unscrewing the panel at the back and showing us the very complicated looking insides, told us to try turning up the small dial which controlled the temperature inside the freezer. Surprisingly, this was something we had already tried but naturally, being English, we didn't like to mention this. He told us to ring again if the freezer continued to be a useless hulk of white taking up a large area of floor space in the pantry. We waited what we thought was a decent time (two days) and then rang the manufacturers again. They sent another engineer who was specifically trained to deal with problems affecting this particular model. He came (with a bigger bag of tools) and, after taking the back off, told us that there was a fault but that he wasn't qualified to deal with it. He said we should telephone the manufacturer and ask them to send another engineer. He said he would send them a report telling them what sort of engineer we needed but warned that it was possible that it might not be possible to mend the freezer satisfactorily. We asked if they would replace the freezer since we had understood that was what the guarantee was for. He said they would want to continue exploring the possibility of repairing the freezer before they would replace it. Wearily, we ordered another freezer from another manufacturer. They brought the replacement in 48 hours and took away the one that didn't work.

'Would you like to purchase the extra warranty?' we were asked.

We said that was very kind of them to offer but that we didn't think we would take them up on their kind offer.

We are constantly told that we should mend things rather than throw them away but stuff is so complicated these days that no one can mend anything. And so the mountains of waste become ever bigger. Or maybe it's just quicker and more profitable to sell a new whatever it is when the old whatever it was stops working.

Integrity has gone missing in most areas of life, largely because there is no accountability. No one in high office ever apologises these days. Politicians never pay the price for their incompetence and failure. Nor do generals, senior doctors, judges, top level civil servants or anyone else in a position of power and authority. If a private soldier loses a boot or, heaven forbid, a rifle he will be court martialled and imprisoned. If a general loses an army and a war he will be promoted or given a well-paid job in a quango. If a senior civil servant costs the tax payers £100 billion, the worst that will happen is an early pension and a seat on the board of some company which wants his contacts book.

Think back over the last few decades. Everywhere you look there is nothing but failure and incompetence, dishonesty and deceit. And even when the liars and cheats have no choice but to resign (a rare occurrence in itself) they suffer hardly at all.

And so our old Bentley is a reassuring reminder of integrity and good workmanship.

But I can't help thinking that it is a good job for most of us that God does not have the same attitude towards quality control as modern manufacturers have, and does not regard the idea of planned obsolescence with such enthusiasm.

The car was away at the garage for several weeks and I chafed at the delay. I felt like a child waiting for Christmas. I was desperate to start driving it.

Three garage mechanics have separately told me that cars like to be used. One told me that the Maserati we bought a month before the lockdowns began in 2020, needed to be given a good thrashing once a week if it was to stay in good condition. It spent most of its early months sitting and waiting. (I should, perhaps, mention that when we bought the car, I was still a bestselling author with books in 26 languages, selling in over 50 countries. And I was one of Amazon's top selling authors. Things have changed since I wrecked my career by committing the 21st crime of sharing uncomfortable truths which the establishment wants suppressed.)

What the mechanics say makes sense. If a car isn't run then the bits and pieces will become stiff and won't work easily. The engine parts need oil to keep them working well and if the engine doesn't run then there won't be any oil going round.

It is, of course, the same with humans. Spend a month in bed and you'll find yourself weak and wobbly when you try to walk.

The problem with the car was not so much getting the work done as finding the parts and then waiting for them to arrive. If you need an ignition box or a section of exhaust pipe for a new Ford or a new Toyota, the garage will probably be able to find the item you need in minutes and have it delivered within hours. They may even have it in stock.

Things don't work like that with really old cars.

Our Bentley had hardly been used for years and so it wasn't surprising that it needed attention. Even the doors were stiff and difficult to open. For quite a while I harboured the bizarre thought that the boot lid had been soldered shut. And the petrol flap wouldn't open until it was eased into action with the aid of a penknife blade. (I promise you that there wasn't the slightest scratch on the paintwork as a result.)

The human body is much the same, of course, and if it isn't used regularly then things gradually stop working. Joints seize up and let you down. And the brain is part of the body and will also slow down if it isn't given a work out occasionally.

I don't know how one old car should feel or drive compared to others of the same age. Will our Bentley be behaving well or will it be struggling?

But I don't know the answer to this question about myself either. Am I doing well for a man in his late seventies or am I deteriorating more or less than the average? Do all men who are my age feel the same as I do? Do they feel stronger, younger and healthier? Or do they feel more worn out? I have no idea. And, of course, it doesn't really matter.

The worst thing most people can do is to go into a care home where they lie in bed or (just as bad) sit in high backed plastic chairs and stare at one another (or the damned television screen) all day long. A pathetic, twenty minute chair bound exercise session once a week (led by a chubby and over cheerful 19-year-old in a sparkly leotard) won't do any damned good.

I hate care homes. I really do. When I was a young GP I had patients in several care homes and I remember that one of the homes (a huge place run by the council) had nowhere at all for residents to exercise but did have the best part of an acre of grass at the front and side of the building. Once a week a council employee with a ride on mower would turn up and cut the grass. There were no paths and no benches and therefore there was nowhere for anyone to walk or sit. There were, however, two 'Keep Off the Grass' signs.

I once asked the manager/matron/governor/headmistress or whatever she was called if it would be possible to allow some of the residents to dig up a patch of grass and create a few allotments where they could grow things – flowers to look at and fruit and vegetables to eat. I explained all the ways in which this would help the residents (many of whom were still quite healthy and though only in their sixties were subsiding rapidly into dependent, institutionalised old age) and how it wouldn't cost the council anything but might save on food bills and grass cutting costs. Gardening would provide residents with physical exercise, a hobby and something to look forward to.

You'd have thought I'd suggested opening a bordello in the East Wing. I was told that it was impractical and quite impossible. The words 'risk' and 'insurance' came up a good deal.

When I repeated the question at regular intervals, a 'meeting' was eventually held. (As a GP with responsibility for the care of a number of residents, it was decided that I was entitled to a 'meeting'.)

I wasn't invited to the meeting but I was told the outcome.

The manager explained that it would be impossible to do as I suggested because there was no one available to supervise the elderly and to make sure that they didn't hurt themselves (or one another) with spades, forks, trowels or other pieces of gardening equipment. Who would take on the responsibility if a resident tripped over a weed and broke a limb? Who would pay for showing the residents how to use their spades safely? Who would deal with complaints from residents' relatives? (I was assured that some residents' relatives would be certain to complain and so where would we be then?)

In the end, bureaucracy won and nothing happened, though I used the story of old people overcoming the bureaucrats and using their spades and rakes and hoes in my novel 'Mrs Caldicot's Knickerbocker Glory', the second of my stories about the wonderful Mrs Caldicot.

My failed attempt to improve my patients' lives took place around 50 years ago and since then researchers have shown that the way we think about ageing, and our attitude towards getting older, can increase our lifespan by seven years. A study of old people organised by the Yale School of Public Health found that older folk who remain positive about themselves, and retain a feeling of being useful, live for an average of another 22.6 years, whereas those who did not feel positive about ageing lived just another 15 years.

Studies have shown that until the age of 90, the normal processes of ageing (as opposed to obvious pathology) have little effect on your ability to function, to get about, to mix with other people and to look after yourself. Disease and a loss of physical or mental function will make you feel weak and old, but simply getting old won't necessarily make you behave as old people are expected to behave.

Naturally, however, it is wise to be aware that when you're 70 you aren't going to be able to run around with all the zip of a 17-

year-old. And you won't recover anywhere near as quickly either. But you can stay fitter if you do regular exercise. Brisk walking, stretching, weight lifting and balancing on one leg can all help delay the consequences of longevity. This is particularly important if you've over 70 years of age. Muscle power tends to decline fairly dramatically if you rest for longer periods after the age of 70. Even people who are convalescing should try to get up and about as quickly as possible. Most people who've had surgery can get up and take light exercise quite soon afterwards.

And, of course, the best way to retain your physical and mental health is to maintain a sense of purpose; to give yourself goals and responsibilities. People who sit around waiting for something to happen will probably find that nothing much happens. It doesn't matter what you do as long as it is something you enjoy. Learning a language or learning how to play a musical instrument will do your brain a massive amount of good.

The bottom line is that human bodies and cars have one vital thing in common: both need to be used. If your body isn't pushed occasionally, but is allowed to spend all day drooping in an arm chair, then you will gradually lose your muscular powers. If you don't push your brain, and use it as hard as you can on a daily basis, then your brain will decay and leave you with a skull full of useless, grey mush. Similarly, motor cars need to be used.

There's something else that cars and people have in common: their propensity to break down if they are messed around with too much. Every car owner knows that cars seem particularly likely to go wrong immediately after they've been serviced. And when a car is returned after a service, it's always annoying to find out how many of the settings have been altered.

Human bodies may not have settings to alter but they too have a tendency to develop faults after a 'service' or a 'check-up'. Most people assume that side effects only occur after treatment (such as taking a drug) but even a simple blood test can produce problems (bleeding, bruising and so on) and some tests produce side effects that take years to appear (too many X-rays can cause a cancer which appears many years later) and more invasive procedures can be lethal. I have known many people who've spent much of their lives at the doctor's, some of them having so much done to them, and spending so much time and money on treatment, that they appear to be staying alive for the sake of staying alive. A worrying number of them have developed serious health issues, and even died, as a result of all this unnecessary fettling.

The danger is exacerbated, of course, because it is rare for a patient to visit a physician or surgeon without the doctor offering some sort of treatment. Doctors are trained to intervene and it should not be any surprise that most, if not quite all, interfere far too often.

Most 67-year-old Bentleys spend their days cocooned in air conditioned garages. They are fettled and fussed over and taken out on fine days. They are towed to competitive meetings when they are compared with other concours condition vehicles. Most old cars travel at most a hundred or so miles a year under their own steam. We believe that our old Bentley should be used as often as possible – and that we shouldn't worry too much about it remaining in perfect condition.

When French writer Honore de Balzac had finished a book, he would write 'The End' at the bottom of the final sheet. He would then reach for a new sheet of paper, dip his quill in his inkwell and write 'Chapter One' at the top of the new sheet of paper. (He'd worry later about the title for the book.) For some that may be the definition of 'workaholic'. For others it is the definition of 'keeping busy'.

I had owned several old Bentleys (and one old Rolls Royce) and although they had always been a great deal of trouble (though to be honest not a great deal more trouble than the new Bentley Continental we owned a few years ago) they were glorious machines to own, drive in and just sit inside. And I wanted to share that joy with Antoinette, who had never even sat in a really old Bentley let alone owned one or travelled anywhere in one.

The sad truth is, of course, that large, old cars of this type are far too big for modern roads and quite unsuitable for today's car parks where the spaces available seem to get narrower every year and the access usually requires the agility of something short and concise. Big cars weren't built for crowded town centres. The turning circle of a Bentley S type is so huge that these cars require a ten acre field if you want to turn them round. Modern car parks have spaces designed to fit pedal cars not real cars.

Driving old cars requires skills which most drivers of modern cars have long forgotten and which drivers under 50 have never acquired. There are no seat belts but there is a button on the floor which you have to press every 200 miles in order to oil the chassis. The steering is almost unbelievably light.

A joy rider would probably crash before he'd travelled ten feet.

There are some good things: there is no need to pay an annual road tax or to have the car examined for an MOT certificate and the costs of insurance are remarkably low. In addition, many cities allow drivers of classic cars to enter without the now standard fee commonly charged to proper cars with internal combustion engines.

MOTs for older cars were abandoned not out of generosity because garages got fed up with the damage being done to their machinery. One mechanic told me that after one MOT it took them hours to clean out the machine used for measuring exhaust smoke. Classic car owners were delighted to see the end of the MOT because garages could at times be quite unreasonable. A Bentley S type which I previously owned failed its annual MOT because of a miniscule crack in one of the headlights. The crack made absolutely no difference to the quality of the beam and it was too small and insignificant to allow water to enter but it took five months to find a replacement glass that would fit, and the car had to kept off the road for all that time. And for the record, a replacement headlamp glass for a classic Bentley costs about the same as you'd pay for an entire Chinese-made electric car.

At slow speeds there is quite a lag with the foot brake which makes the brakes pretty useless and so manoeuvring and parking require steady, skilful use of the handbrake. This isn't just a problem with our Bentley: all S type cars are the same in this respect. The car is so long that the front end and the back end can easily appear to be in different counties. The wing mirrors and tiny driving mirror seem to be there as decorations rather than as visual aids and naturally there is no reversing camera. Nor are there any buzzing sensors to warn you that you're about to bump into another car or a gatepost. Visibility is poor, though the road holding is excellent. You can throw the car round corners and roundabouts like a sports car. If you get much more than 10-12 mpg then you're either driving like an old lady with myopia and a light foot or you're still parked. (The petrol tank takes 18 gallons and an early complaint was that the car needed refuelling every 200-250 miles. Still, back in the 1950s and 1960s there were plenty of petrol stations around.) Climate change enthusiasts should remember that one of these cars is two thirds of a century old, and is therefore infinitely better for the environment than one which came out of a factory months ago, and then had to be transported half way across the world on a container ship.

Each year that arrives, human beings use more and more stuff. As humans we spend much of our time and money digging big holes in the ground and removing minerals. The minerals are used to make 'things'. When we decide we've got enough use out of them, or they break down, the 'things' are tossed aside, some bits and pieces are salvaged, and the remainder dumped into big holes that have been dug in the ground.

A still functioning 67-year-old car is the perfect example of how we should use our natural resources. Modern petrol and diesel cars do well if they last ten years. They are badly made and over complicated and therefore too expensive to repair.

Modern electric cars last no more than five or six years before they are worthless and someone has to find a way to get rid of all those batteries. Every way you look at them electric cars are of little or no value: they are of no real value to individuals and they are certainly of no value to the planet and the environment. They are, however, fashionable. In a year or two, when huge numbers of electric cars have to be thrown away, the world is going to find itself with a huge problem of what to do with them all.

Cars like our elderly Bentley were built to last a lifetime and are, for those who worry about these things, far friendlier to the environment than modern cars which have a very limited life span. Our Bentley will, I suspect, be around much longer than I shall be able to drive it. When I'm gone it will go, I sincerely hope, to someone who will also cherish it and enjoy it as a motor car rather than a stagnant work of art. Old cars are like houses that were built more than half a century ago. Those old houses will last for centuries more (if the authorities don't bulldoze them out of politically inspired spite) and the same is true of cars built more than half a century ago. We are merely custodians, rather than owners.

You can learn a good deal by looking (and I mean really 'looking') at old artefacts.

Standing in our hallway we have a 17th century long-case clock (of the style usually described as a 'grandfather clock'). The clock is unusual in that it has just one hand.

Visitors who see the clock usually assume that one of the hands (the minute hand) has fallen off and been lost.

But there was never a minute hand.

Back in the 17th century, people didn't worry about the minutes. They weren't constantly in a rush to catch a train or get to an airport four hours early in order to get through security. It was good enough for them to know that the time was around a quarter past four or approximately half past five.

These days we rush about catching trains, missing aeroplanes and racing to make appointments. We put ourselves under constant pressure in this way.

But at the same time as we are struggling to save time, we are also wasting time in prodigious quantities.

The most absurd example of this is the internet.

We tend to think of the internet as a time saving innovation. And it can be. But most of the time the internet wastes time in huge quantities. We send endless quantities of emails. And we receive them in terrifying quantities. Buying a new freezer recently involved 12 emails from the seller. And once the freezer had arrived we received a hail of emails telling us that the machine had arrived, and asking us if we are happy.

A week ago I went through my email box and unsubscribed from all the newsletters to which I appear to have subscribed. (I suspect that most of them were simply junk mail masquerading as newsletters). I marked every email that wasn't important as spam. And since I did that, I've saved at least half an hour a day. If I receive too many junk emails at an email address then I kill that address and open another. It's too easy to waste an hour or two a day looking at, and deleting, unwanted emails. Too many companies bombard you daily, or twice daily, with emails and then sell your address to a dozen 'associate companies' who do the same thing. (An 'associate' company seems to be one that will pay the original company a fat fee for a list of customers' email addresses.)

Now that I am into extra time, I am constantly aware of how easy it is to waste minutes and hours and I am, therefore, always looking for ways to avoid wasting time. So, for example, I don't put the grass box onto the mower because if I do that it will take me twice as long to cut the lawn. If I leave the cuttings where they fall, they will soon become part of the lawn and the grass will be healthier. If a clump of cuttings appears, I just use the rake to spread them about. In the summer this saves me around eight hours. That's an extra day for sitting in the garden, reading a book and enjoying the view.

Looking back I seem to have spent my life in a hurry and I now have difficulty remembering where the time went. It's a blur. I feel angry with myself for all the wasted years, months, weeks, days, hours and minutes. I feel angry about all the time wasted on crap – usually crap emanating from other people's demands. The endless wasted moments accumulate and congeal into waste lands of wasted time. I have become more aware of this wastage as I have become older.

Look after the minutes and the hours will look after themselves.

Look back a few decades and it is astonishing to see just how much people managed to get done before the internet, email and bureaucracy took hold of our lives and ate up the minutes, the hours, the days and the years without our having any say in the matter.

John Buchan, who wrote such splendid novels as 'Thirty Nine Steps' and 'John McNab', qualified as a lawyer, worked as a diplomat and became a partner at one of London's major publishing houses. He was also editor of 'The Spectator' and the father of four children. He worked as a correspondent in France for 'The Times' in the First World War and held a field commission in the Intelligence Corps. He was the Government's Director of Information and President of various societies. He was an MP and a significant figure in the Church of Scotland. When he was appointed Governor General of Canada, he became Lord Tweedsmuir. He collected a huge number of awards and honours and held three honorary military appointments. In addition to writing 29 extremely successful novels, he wrote 11 major biographies, four collections of poetry, six collections of short stories and 66 other non-fiction books. He also edited 14 books. He often had poor health and was just 64-years-old when he died.

I doubt if he would have been able to cram quite so much into a fairly short life if he'd also had to deal with hundreds of emails and read his own gas and electricity meters.

The S type Bentley weighs over two tons, has an engine capacity of nearly five litres and is the best part of 18 feet long. When new, it managed 12-14 miles per gallon if you drove it carefully. There is a leather sofa disguised as a bench seat in the front (for the driver and a couple of passengers) and another sofa in the back. There is a complex heating and ventilation system, a rear window demister, two perfectly matched mahogany picnic tables in the back and one in the front. Everything is made of wood or metal or leather. I suppose there must be unnatural materials in there somewhere but I haven't found any yet. The car has an imperious air which, on narrow country lanes, results in vans, lorries, buses and even tractors backing up and reversing into gateways and ditches to get out of the way. You think I'm exaggerating, but I'm not.

When the Bentley S type was first launched in the mid-1950s, it was described by motoring journalists (who all drooled over it) as 'a brisk, mobile drawing room', 'the best car in the world' and 'the fastest luxury car ever manufactured'. And brisk it was for the time. Described as a 'sports saloon' the Bentley S type was one of the first production cars capable of exceeding 100 mph and capable of doing it all day long without a murmur of protest. Tony Brooks, the former FI grand prix winner and the grand prix drivers' driver of choice, drove an early model the whole north-south length of France, covering a gazillion miles in less than a day, including a lengthy stop for luncheon and inevitable halts to replenish the petrol tank. These are, after all, large sports cars. Bentley motor cars have a marvellous sporting history, with the marque's success at Le Mans in the 1920s being the stuff of legends galore. Marvellous books have been written about the Bentley Boys – amateur drivers who epitomised a time now lost, but never to be forgotten.

In most respects the S type Bentley is exactly the same vehicle as the Rolls Royce Silver Cloud. The engine, the chassis and most of the bodywork is the same. The only real difference is the badge on the bonnet. The Silver Cloud has the flying lady mascot on her bonnet while the Bentley S type has a (slightly differently shaped) bonnet decorated with a stately looking flying B. There were three manifestations of both cars and although the variations are now known as the Bentley S1, S2 and S3 the first model was simply known as the S type for the simple, rational reason that you can't call something an S1 until you know that there are going to be an S2 and an S3.

Why did we choose to buy an S type Bentley? Why a Bentley and not, say, an old Rolls Royce, an old Aston Martin, an old Riley or an old Something Else?

Well, not buying an old Rolls Royce was easy. For me the marque, I'm afraid, is now too closely allied with royalty, sheiks, arms dealers, slimy financiers and Arthur Daley of Minder infamy. There's a grubbiness about modern Rolls Royce motor cars that has never tarnished Bentley. Rolls Royce reached its apogee in the 1920s and 1930s, and it is a 20/25 model from that era which is driven by the doctor in my 'Young Country Doctor' series of books set in the 1970s.

The S1 Bentley was, by popular agreement (both among those who love motor cars and those who simply love beautiful artefacts), the last truly great car; a symbol of what was once admirable.

That's why we wanted to own one.

And a car built in the 1950s should, I thought (with exceptional and unusual optimism), be practical enough to drive and to use on a regular basis. The Bentley S1 marked the point when cars were built with useful driver aids (an automatic gear box and power steering for example) but without the often unnecessary driver aids which are fitted to modern cars. Manufacturers and eager owners often seem to forget that the more there is to go wrong, the more will go wrong.

My only niggle is that the back doors can only be opened by reaching around over the back of the front seats. Anyone with short arms would find it impossible. And since there are no safety locks, the back doors can easily be opened by leaning on the handle. (I did this when travelling in an old Morris when I was about five. I leant on the handle and fell out of the car onto the road. Fortunately, we were travelling very slowly. My Dad immediately made and fitted a locking device to the back doors.)

I knew that if things turned out badly then the downside wasn't too bad. We could always sit in the back seat and have a picnic. This sounds bizarre and I can't really begin to explain but I'd be happy to sit in it even if it didn't move. The unique smell of the mahogany and the leather, with an undertone of engine oil, the feel and the textures, nourish the soul and satisfy a quiet yearning for stability; they give strength to the part of the soul which requires a haven away from the exhausting traumas of the 21st century.

Everything about the S1 is the antithesis of the mean world we now inhabit. It is far removed from the digital future we are threatened with, full of nasty apps and horrid electric cars, designed and built with as much passion as milk carts and trundled off the conveyor belt with a yawn.

The Bentley S type was the last elegant, refined, graceful and dignified vehicle ever made. It was, and is, opulent but tasteful. It could never be thought regal or ostentatious. It was the choice of sportsmen and those who either had a little money to indulge themselves or who were prepared to do without other things in order to purchase one.

There is a widespread assumption that new must mean better. New cars, fitted with all the bells and whistles their designers can dream up, and enough computing power to send a rocket to the moon and back, are automatically assumed to be 'better', in some rarely defined way, than old cars which don't have electric windows, sensors to turn on the windscreen wipers if a drop of rain falls on the windscreen, sensors to switch on the lights if it gets dusk (and dip them if a car approaches) and devices to enable the police to track the car if it is stolen or even to bring the stolen car to a halt if a thief is making his getaway.

We have a 1957 Bentley, a Mitsubishi L200 truck and a modern Maserati. Putting aside the truck (which we have for when the weather is bad and the roads very wet or icy) which of them is better?

Well, I hate to say it, and I hope that the Maserati isn't reading this (which it probably could do if it wanted to) but the Bentley is easier and more fun to drive. Inevitably, it has few of the gadgets which are fitted because they are supposed to make life easier but which can all too easily go wrong and make life more difficult.

The Maserati has so much electric stuff going on all the time that the battery is constantly running down. To avoid problems, the battery has to be connected to the mains every 14 days or so. And here's the killer: the battery is stored in the boot and I can only open the boot by using a button on the key. If the battery is flat the only way to get at the battery is to find a mechanic who is prepared and able to remove the back seats and climb into the boot. He must, of course, be small enough and agile enough to do this.

The 67-year-old Bentley also keeps its battery in the boot but when the ignition is switched off that's it. The car shuts down until I need it again. And if the battery does go flat and needs attention I simply open the boot, with a small, metal object called a key, and either replace the battery or attach some jump leads.

Cars aren't the only things that have got too complicated. The obsession with what is thought of as progress is widespread. Everyone, everywhere, seems to be constantly searching for something new.

In 1977, I wrote a book called Paper Doctors in which I argued that the obsession with medical research had got out of control. I pointed out that we already had masses of useful information about preventing diseases, detecting diseases and treating diseases but that we used only a tiny proportion of that information because all medical scientists and most practising doctors in academic circles were far too busy looking for new information to store away in university libraries to have time to use the information we already have.

I argued that the world would be much better off if all scientists stopped all their medical research and, instead, put their energies into finding ways to use the information we have but have never used.

Naturally, the argument was not enthusiastically received. Scientists, and academic doctors, are paid to do research. And they receive awards and honours and bonuses if they find something new – whether or not it is of any practical value. No one cares if new information is useful. All they care about is: 'Is this new?'

What is true of cars and medicine is true about everything else, too.

For example, historians looking back at World War II often seem to think that the V-2 rockets devised by Germany were (almost) a game changer. But they weren't. In both military and economic terms the V-2 rockets were a huge waste of money. More people died making the V-2 rockets than were killed by them. A single raid using old-fashioned bombers, and old-fashioned bombs would have done far more damage than all the V-2 rockets put together.

The same is true of the atomic bomb. If the money and effort used to create the atom bomb had been used in making and dropping old-fashioned bombs, the effect would have been far more catastrophic. (And people wouldn't have been dying decades later as a result of the fallout.)

And here's the killer: one of the most useful weapons in World War II was the horse.

The United States Army's 10th Mountain Division used more than ten thousand horses and mules, and George S. Patton, an enthusiastic tank general, confessed that he wished that he had had more horses. Horses and mules can carry huge loads, they are reliable, they are not terribly expensive and they can traverse ground that is impassable for tanks.

If the money spent on creating the Atom bomb had been spent on acquiring more horses and mules then World War II would have probably been over more quickly.

Our Bentley's restoration bills added up quickly, as I knew they would, of course. To the £15,000 purchase price, the £2250 auctioneer's commission and the £1,000 fee for the transporter to bring the car from the auction rooms to our home we had to add: £300 insurance (which came with free membership of the RAC motoring organisation)

£134.20 for the driver's manual (almost certainly the best owner's handbook ever produced for anything, anywhere)
£39 for spare keys
£207 for a transporter to take the car to the garage
£204 for a transporter to take the car to the garage a second time
£105.50 for a battery
£429 for a master cylinder
£429 for a another master cylinder (only one of the brakes' master cylinders was leaking but it seemed wise to repair both)
£450 for a power steering ram
£320 for a rear silencer
£468 for an ignition box (I was refunded £100 because we sent back the old ignition box and received a payment for that – the supplier, Flying Spares, will recondition the old one and sell it to someone else)
£31 for leather patches for when we get round to effecting a temporary repair
£7 for a pot of touch up paint which we don't need yet
£588.5 for a reconditioned radiator (we received a discount on the price by sending back our original radiator which needed work because it had been left without coolant and was damaged and rusty; the radiator that was in the car had been rebuilt in 2018 but had not been cleaned out or properly maintained)
£33.50 for the carriage for the radiator
£37.75 for antifreeze for the radiator
£193.47 for a new thermostat
£107.95 for a steam valve
£350 for various washers, gaskets, fluids, oils, hoses, clips, seals and other bits and pieces far too boring to detail
Plus costs to the garage for labour
And £176 for a custom built cover to fit the car (not yet used because it looks a lot of trouble, and I subsequently read somewhere that putting a cover on a car can cause more problems than it solves)
£0 road tax
£0 MOT

Since the car is in considerably better condition now than it was when we bought it, I've upped the insurance to £30,000.

So, what sort of tinny, modern vehicle could we have bought for £30,000?

The Bentley's power steering RAM has had to be replaced. I have no idea what this is or what it does but I'm trying to look as though I know what I'm writing about.

Whenever I tell people that a 1957 car has power steering, they are impressed. The power steering broke on my previous S type Bentley and I drove for over 200 miles with part of the mechanism waving about inside the engine bay. This could, apparently, have been disastrous. But it wasn't. I did, however, find it incredibly hard work to steer the car without power assistance. These days I very much doubt if I'd be able to turn the wheel at all if the power steering went while I was driving.

While the car was away at the garage having essential work done to make it entirely roadworthy, I spent my time doing a little research. I managed to buy (for £50) a huge loose-leaf workshop manual packed with illustrated instructions on how to maintain and repair the car. I didn't buy this in the expectation that I would be able to do my own maintenance (I don't have the basic knowledge, the skills, the patience, the tools, or a properly equipped garage with a pit and a hoist) but in the hope that I would at least have a rough idea what we were talking about when I discussed the work to be done with the garage. I did hope that if I looked at the manual I would know what the garage mechanics were telling me. However, I confess I have not yet had more than a cursory look at it, partly because it looks rather daunting, partly because it is a very large loose-leaf folder and partly because it is second hand and smeared with oil marks; it does however look enormously impressive and if I am called upon to discuss repair work with an engineer, I shall hold the manual in front of me with considerable aplomb, in the hope that he will suspect, if not believe, that I know what he is talking about.

Up until a couple of decades ago, even men who would not describe themselves as experts on cars would repair and tinker with their vehicles, usually in their driveway on a Sunday morning. It was, for many, an enjoyable hobby and an opportunity to do something to make their car a little different. Today, cars are so complex that it has become impossible even for professional car mechanics to do anything without the ubiquitous computer. I remember being shocked a few years ago when a breakdown mechanic came to look at our Mitsubishi L200 truck. He was dressed more like an accountant than a car mechanic, and the first thing he did when he arrived was connect a laptop computer to the car and run some sophisticated tests. This enabled him to tell me that the car would have to be taken to the garage to be repaired. I got the impression that he could probably change a wheel or connect jump leads to the battery to start the car (as long as the computer approved) but that there wasn't much else he could do.

Computers and modern technology have made it impossible for a bloke with a box full of spanners to do anything useful to a car (or any other piece of equipment for that matter) and even fully equipped garages seem to be limited to removing parts of the car and replacing them, rather than repairing faulty items. So, for example, if a wing mirror is damaged the whole unit has to be discarded and replaced, and when windscreen wipers stop working properly the unit has to be replaced, rather than just putting in a pair of new wiper blades which might have cost no more than a couple of quid. The waste is phenomenal.

There are vital things to be learnt about ourselves, our bodies, our health and our attitude to life from dealing with old motor cars.

Our 1957 Bentley has a number of faults. So, for example, the temperature gauge doesn't seem to work properly. After driving for a few miles the needle on the gauge rises into the red zone and stays there. The wise man at the garage looked at this and found a problem with the radiator, which had become clogged after years of little or no use. He put in a new radiator but found that this didn't solve the problem with the temperature gauge. The fact is that the water temperature only appears to be hot and the problem, it seems, lies not in the radiator but in the transmitter carrying appropriate messages about the temperature from the gauge on the dashboard. And I was not surprised to hear that there is, or appears to be, something of a shortage of suitable replacement transmitters for 67-year-old motor cars.

The answer, I decided, is to ignore the gauge and to rely on other warning signs. So, if steam or bubbling hot water appears from the radiator then I will stop the car, wait for it to cool down and then drive home slowly. I can manage without a temperature gauge.

The problem hasn't been cured but it has been side stepped.

Similarly the petrol tank gauge doesn't work. The needle is stuck permanently at half full. I could take the car to the garage and leave it there for weeks or months while the mechanics hunt around online and find a replacement for the part of the gauge that isn't working properly, and then fit the replacement.

Or I could just make a note of the reading on the mileometer when I buy petrol, and buy more petrol when I've done 180 miles or so. Since I already have to make a note of the mileage in order to know when to press the button to oil the chassis, this is no great problem. The trip meter is frozen but the mileometer still works (the car has done 59,000 miles since 1957) so keeping an eye on the mileage won't be difficult.

The small lockable compartment (known as the glove box to most people though Bentley call it a 'cubby box') on the passenger side of the front of the car should lock but it doesn't because the lock mechanism seems to be broken. Who cares? I have had dozens of cars with glove boxes which locked and I don't think I have ever locked one in my life. The locks are usually fairly fragile and no match for a determined thief armed with a screwdriver.

What I am doing, of course, is merely adapting my life, and my expectations, to the car's deficiencies. I am working around the problems rather than confronting them head on. If I take the car into the garage every time I find a fault then I will have very little time to enjoy driving it. At the end of two years I will probably have a pretty well perfect (and expensively restored) vehicle but I will have had very little fun with it. It's too easy to own an old car which becomes the motorised equivalent of an old rock group – still blasting along, making a little noise when this seems appropriate, but having few of the original parts.

And it occurs to me that maybe this is a philosophy which we should apply to our own bodies.

As we age we all lose some of our flexibility, strength and skills. Nothing works quite as well as it did when we were 20-years-old. It is, of course, possible to get something done about most of the things that are faulty, or not working as efficiently as they did previously, but that can mean making quite a sacrifice in terms of time, pain and money. And there are risks in having surgery or taking pills.

I obviously don't know what feeling old is supposed to feel like (since it's nothing I've done before) but there are inevitably going to be consequences as the machinery becomes worn.

People deal with ageing in very different ways. And their expectations are important.

I was with my father, when he was in his mid-80s, when he told a consultant physician (rather indignantly) that he couldn't walk up hills as easily as he had once been able to do. 'What are you going to do about it?' demanded my father.

The consultant looked at my father in astonishment and then looked at me rather pleadingly. I explained to my father that he would just have to be prepared to walk a little less rapidly, and to rest a while from time to time.

(Unfortunately, I wasn't always with my father when he saw a doctor, and after he died my wife and I had to take two large black bags full of prescribed pills to the pharmacist. It was, in fact, the prescription drugs which eventually killed him. Actually, it wasn't so much the drugs which killed him as the careless and ignorant doctor who had prescribed them.)

Many people find it difficult to accept that things aren't going to work as well when they age.

A neighbour told me (with considerable pride) that he and his wife between them had four new knees and three new shoulders fitted. (I always feel surprised that whereas the knee joints we were given at the start of our lives can usually last 70 plus years before showing signs of wear and tear, the expensively crafted artificial joints which are provided as replacements last only a few years.) Neither the man nor his wife was in great pain before their surgery and they could both get around quite well, though he sometimes used a walking stick.

I find it strange that anyone would rather go through the pain, risk and expense of major surgery to avoid the relatively mild inconvenience of using a walking stick.

Many people's lives are occupied by a constant search for surgery and new treatments as they fight the daily battle against decaying teeth, increasing deafness, constant indigestion, breathlessness, pain in every joint, backache, palpitations, forgetfulness, poor circulation, leg ulcers, hair loss, high blood pressure, skin discolorations and more. Millions go to an optician every six months to have their eyes tested, and to a dentist every six months to have their teeth and gums assessed. They have regular bowel, breast and heart checks. The slightest abnormality must be investigated at length and then treated (also at length) with the side effects of the treatment then requiring more tests and more treatments. Patients in their 60s and older are often taking a dozen or more different types of drug every day. They need charts and special pill dispensers to help them keep a check on what they have taken and what they need to take. Even varicose veins suddenly need attention. I knew a woman well into her seventies who insisted on having surgery performed on her hardly visible varicose veins. Dodgy knees, elbows, shoulders and hips need regular testing. There are endless procedures to be undertaken and regular screenings to be endured. There are injections to have and vaccinations galore to protect against the flu, shingles and a range of disorders. These constant visits to doctors and other health professionals create a sense of victimhood and passivity which the health professionals encourage. Regular praise is offered to those who remember their name and age correctly. On top of the orthodox care provided, alternative practitioners use the mainstream media and the internet to provide advice and answers for every known ailment, and some ailments that have not yet been defined.

It is no big surprise that no one over the age of eighteen wants to be older and many over the age of 50 have started working out how many days of life they might have left. In the country of the old there is no normal. It's perhaps no surprise that suicide is highest among those over the age of 75.

I read a book the other day in which the author, no older than I am, confessed that she spent 80% of her time visiting doctors and clinics of one sort or another and that her friends thought that this was fairly normal. Gore Vidal called his final years 'the hospital years'. There are well over a million people over the age of 80 currently living in the UK, and if they all spend most of their time queuing to see a doctor then it is hardly surprising that the queues are unmanageable.

(It is generally assumed that the world is full of old people because doctors and drug companies have extended the average life.

This is, however, a myth. And it is a myth which is carefully sustained by self-serving doctors and drug company executives who claim that life expectancy has risen dramatically in recent years as a result of the work of doctors and drug companies. Sadly, this is a myth created to excuse the garbage sold by drug companies and prescribed by doctors. There are two reasons why it seems that we're living longer. First, there are more people alive today than fifty years ago. And so there are bound to be more old people around. Second, mortality figures are skewed by the fact that at the end of the 19th century, infant mortality rates were incredibly high. Babies died regularly of cholera and other infectious diseases. Today, most babies live. Every baby who dies when a few months old drags down the average life expectation. If more babies live then the average goes up. And babies are now more likely to live not because of the drug industry or doctors but because of cleaner drinking water, cleaner air, better sewage disposal and so on.)

But if you live another ten years and spend eight of them in hospitals or doctors' waiting rooms you are arguably worse off than someone who lived another three years without bothering with doctors. And, of course, this ignores the pain, discomfort, cost and inconvenience of all the treatments that will be offered and doubtless accepted. There is no drug or surgical treatment that does not come without side effects. There is no screening procedure that is 100% accurate or reliable. I'm afraid that doctors and drug companies have a distinct tendency to oversell themselves and their products.

All this emphasis on illness and treatment means that most old people spend their days moaning about their ailments, talking about their friend's ailments, attending funerals, remembering those who have gone, (feeling good about still being here) and abandoning all their hopes and plans because it becomes impossible to fit hobbies and interests in between all the hospital and doctor appointments.

It seems to me that the elderly are entitled to have a little more fun. As the responsibilities and obligations have lessened a little (maybe) then the time has come to be more daring and adventurous; to stop worrying about what other people think and to take on new challenges. It seems to me that there isn't much point to being older if all you do is try to repair, to restore and to delay the inevitable aging process. Keeping occupied with projects that are a challenge, and fun to do, seems to me to be the only way to meander through old age with any sense of self-respect and purpose.

I am always astonished by people who want to retire at the age of 50 or 55 (or even earlier) and who genuinely seem to think that they will be satisfied if they spend their remaining years sitting on the beach, sipping cocktails and playing an occasional round of golf. I wonder how many of those who embark on a long, long retirement doing nothing eventually find themselves fading away from boredom and a lack of a challenge. Retirement is an entirely artificial concept and it's important to remember that when pensions were invented in Germany, the age of 65 was chosen as the official retirement age because that was, at the time, the average age of death in Germany. In my experience, loafing is only enjoyable if you have a great deal to do.

And only if you don't entirely fill your days with doctors' appointments, visits to the dentist and the optician, sessions with a physiotherapist and so on, can there possibly be time to take on the sort of projects that are worthy.

The problems of being older are exacerbated by the fact that the elderly are often discarded or rejected merely because of their age.

So, for example, numerous extremely successful authors have had to start publishing their own work because agents and publishers see elderly writers as being of no value.

On the other hand, there are no limits to what can be done once the plunge has been taken. Lawrence Block, one of America's most successful thriller writers, has become one of the world's most successful self-publishers. He is not alone.

The comparison with my old Bentley seems to me to be a solid one. If I leave it at the restorers to be repaired I'll never get any fun out of it.

If I had a pain which kept me awake at night and which wrecked my days, I would try to have something done about it. But if I could find a way around it then I would.

When I was a young house surgeon, I worked for a consultant surgeon who specialised in treating patients with intermittent claudication. This is a condition in which patients have poor circulation and when they walk a good distance, particularly up hill, they tend to get pain in their calves. This is simply a result of the accumulation of waste products in the muscles. The pain disappears if the patient pauses and stands for a moment.

Every day I saw patients who were told that they needed an operation to solve their symptoms. The operation then involved by-passing blocked arteries with veins which were removed from the leg and then grafted onto arteries. It was an operation which normally takes several hours but the surgeon with whom I worked was slow and meticulous and his operations often took twelve hours or more. There would be three shifts of nurses. And the consultant himself would take a break in the middle of the operation. Only the house surgeon (me) was expected to stand at the operating table throughout the procedure. A good number of the surgeon's patients died. They either died on the operating table or they died on the ward a few hours later. Patients who need this operation are never in the best of health, and the mortality rate goes up if they need to be anaesthetised for long periods.

As I became more experienced, I talked to the patients before their operations and tried to explain the risk of the operation. I explained to the frail, and most at risk, that if they merely rested when their pain arrived then the pain would disappear and they would be able to carry on walking. I actually succeeded in persuading a couple of patients to decide not to have the operation. I pointed out to them that if they bought bicycles they would be able to go where they were heading without any pain in their legs. The surgeon, puzzled as to why patients changed their minds, never knew that it was my fault.

The point is that sometimes surgery can be avoided; sometimes there is a way round the problem.

In this respect my attitude to the human body, and my attitude towards it, isn't far removed from my attitude to our 1957 Bentley.

I have accepted that things won't always work efficiently and I try to make the best of it.

I put up with the disappointments.

Buying and enjoying an old car has helped me realise how comparable the ageing process of a car is with the ageing process of a human. Or, rather, how our reaction to the two processes is comparable.

More than that, of course, having an old, classic car has made me look at how our expectations and assumptions are often faulty. Is it really necessary to have a car which turns on its own windscreen wipers when it rains? Is it necessary to have an operation on a slightly worn joint or is a walking stick a better alternative?

The car has helped me re-evaluate the world, my life and the assumptions, attitudes and beliefs we tend to take for granted.

When the Bentley S type (and its twin sister car the Rolls Royce Silver Cloud) were reviewed by motoring journalists, one specialist writer commented that the car was so quiet that the only thing you could hear was the clock ticking. The company's response was, allegedly, to work on making the clock quieter.

Today, even after 67 years, the car is as quiet inside as one of those awful electric cars. But it isn't a silent killer, like electric cars, because those outside can hear a soft, purr like sound – rather like a contented old cat.

And we don't have to worry about the noise of the clock on the dashboard because it makes no sound whatsoever.

It stopped at 4.35 some while ago. It is, of course, an analogue clock and so we have no way of knowing if it stopped in the afternoon or the middle of the night. This is one small mystery which will never be solved.

We are not inclined to have the clock repaired or replaced.

If I want to know the time, I have a £4 watch which I bought on eBay. Finding and replacing the car's clock would probably take another few weeks, involve complicated repair work and cost a small fortune. (I invariably wear my £4 watch because it keeps better time than my expensive watch. When the battery expires it would be cheaper to throw the watch away and buy another because a battery replacement will cost more than twice the price of the watch. But I'll try to take the back off and insert a new button battery myself.)

We needed new batteries for the Bentley and for the Maserati. The new battery for the Maserati cost £398.80 and we were charged £117.00 to have the battery fitted. The total cost of the new battery for the Bentley (including the cost of fitting it) was £105.50.

The garage boss brought the Bentley back today after it had been made safe to use.

'You know,' he said, looking at the car admiringly as he spoke. 'This might not have been a bad buy.' (Though, he didn't know what we paid for it.)

I felt very proud on behalf of the car and not a little pleased with myself.

And I had a lovely surprise: the garage owner agreed to let me pay him with a cheque!

When I expressed delight and surprise, he admitted that the bank costs for putting through a cheque would be smaller than they would have been if I had paid the bill with a credit or debit card. I wish more business folk would realise this and go back to accepting cheques in payment.

Meanwhile, the obliteration of cash continues apace. Bank branches are closing everywhere. And cheques are, we are often told, too dangerous to use. After a few people had cheques stolen and altered, those still using them were warned about the dangers. The message was clear: do all your banking online 'where there are no crooks at all and everything is safe' (that's a joke, by the way). Worse still, cheques are sometimes bounced for absolutely no reason at all (even when there is plenty of money in the relevant account) and it is difficult not to assume that this is being done to make cheque writers agree to go online.

Frighteningly, the majority of people don't seem to care. They love being able to pay their bills with their cards (by waving a card in the air above the card reader) or with their watches. They have no idea of the problems which will ensue. There will be even less privacy, those who don't have access to the internet or fancy banking accounts will be left out of society; there will be massive security risks, and those who upset the authorities in some way will have their accounts frozen. (This already happens with companies such as PayPal which use their ability to turn accounts 'off' as a political weapon). And of course the whole financial system becomes increasingly vulnerable to attack.

The day we got the car back from the garage we took it for a drive. It was a slightly surreal experience. Some people waved. Some took photographs. I could sense that the car was preening slightly, enjoying itself and delighted to be back in service.

There are still things which need doing to the Bentley, of course, though there is no hurry.

We all need a little care and attention as we get older. Some problems can be ignored or lived around. Others are easy to fix.

There is a tear in the leather on the front, bench seat which needs a repair. Maybe we'll bite the bullet and have the front and back seats reupholstered. In the end that might be better, though the smell of old leather combines so well with the smell of many gallons of oil is perhaps too wonderful to risk. The temperature gauge is faulty and wrongly suggests that the car is overheating when it isn't. (Within five minutes of setting off, the needle hits the overheating mark.) The clock still doesn't work, of course, though we don't much care about that. The one shot system for oiling the chassis is leaking as is the differential input seal. The near side front damper unit is leaking and the body mounts are perished. There is some corrosion to the body above the offside rear mounting point. The front ARB drop link bushes are perished. (I have no idea what these are but mentioning them is surely worth at least one brownie point and gives me gravitas I now clearly do not deserve.) None of these faults makes the car unsafe or uncomfortable and we can live with them all.

We only have one key for the ignition but as long as I don't lose that key we'll be fine. The front passenger door still doesn't lock very easily. We need new rubber blades for our windscreen wipers. (If your wiper blades are worn on a modern car you'll probably have to buy the whole assembly. On older cars you could just buy the rubber bit that did the actual wiping.) The horn stopped working for a while and I thought it probably needed a new fuse but then I discovered that there is a spare horn (with a button on the fascia). And then, as soon as I discovered the spare horn button, the horn in the centre of the steering wheel started to work again. It is, as you might expect, a most imperious horn which makes a sound which demands respect without being showy or in any way aggressive.

All I can say in defence of the car is that my own personal 'machine' is suffering from a far longer list of deteriorations and ailments (I won't bother you with them here) and if all any of us has to worry about as we grow older is a little corrosion and a few minor leaks here and there we would be quite content.

All my life I have tried to control the amount of stuff I possess. I have given tens of thousands of books to charity and I've donated vast amounts of furniture and many clothes to such shops. I've even tried selling stuff I didn't want at auction.

The idea that one should throw away an item of clothing for every one you buy was popular for a while and I tried to do the same thing with books.

But it didn't work. I couldn't do it.

I now have so many books and so many DVDS that time and time again I've ended up buying another copy of a book I cannot find or wrongly think I must have given to a charity shop. The same thing is true of DVDs.

I really need to give myself a six month sabbatical so that I can have some new bookcases installed and put all my books into categories.

But, of course, it's not going to happen.

And now we have a Bentley S type too – a motor car which we certainly didn't need.

But which is a delight.

One of the many good things about driving in a Bentley (and there are many) is that there is plenty of room to wear a hat.

When I was young it was rare to see men out of doors without hats. My Dad pretty always wore hats, though usually just one at a time. Men wore hats because they kept their heads warm and protected them from rain and sunburn. Look at old black and white photographs and you'll see that all the men pictured were wearing hats. At the end of a sporting event, the crowd would stream onto the pitch and, if they had something to celebrate, hurl their hats high into the air. (I've wondered how on earth they all found the right hat afterwards. The melee must have been quite something. Can you imagine all the arguments? Maybe they all put their names in their hats in those days.)

Today, the oldest shop in London is a hat shop (Lock and Co of St James Street) and an excellent emporium it is too. In the 1930's over 70 million hats were made every year in England and there were over 500 hat makers in Luton alone. Today hats have pretty well disappeared. I blame the motor car. Tiny modern motor cars are so cramped that there isn't room for a hat as well as a head and so most motorists gave up their hats. I have always tried to buy cars that are high enough to cope with a head with a hat on it.

I wonder if wearing a hat is just something old people do. If so, the future for hatters must be bleak.

I'm not sure but I have always worn a hat when venturing out into the world and I have quite a collection. In the winter I wear warm hats (I have a large variety) and in the summer I wear Panama hats.

I noticed recently that my hats were blowing off my head in the slightest of breezes. Moreover, if I bent down my hat fell off. Since it seemed unlikely that all my hats were getting larger, it seemed likely that my skull was getting smaller. And that is exactly what is happening, of course. It's something that happens as we get older. It isn't the brain that is shrinking (I'm relieved to say) but the bones. The only remedy is to buy new hats. Or I suppose I could put a lining in every hat so that there is a closer fit.

The shrinking of the skull is a normal, but little known part of the ageing process (the gaps between the bones shrinks and the skull gets smaller, just as the same thing happens in the spine with the result that we all get shorter as we age) but it does annoy me that I now have a large collection of hats which no longer fit me properly.

If I buy a complete set of new hats then I fear I'll never get the wear out of them, as my Mother might have said. And what market will there be, even in charity shops, for second-hand hats?

Moreover, if I do buy new ones should I try to estimate how much my head will shrink over the next year or two before purchasing?

Oh, to hell with it, I'll keep the hats I've got.

It isn't just cars which are built not to last these days.

Houses are built to fall down.

You may think this surprising since houses in the UK have never been as unaffordable as they are now (though apparently there was a bubble in 1876 when houses were a little over priced).

House prices were for decades between three and five times annual earnings. Today, house prices are around 10 or more times annual earnings. And, as a result, twice as many 18-34 year olds live with their parents as live independently.

But the irony (and these days there always seems to be some irony involved) is that modern, expensive houses are built to last twenty or thirty years and to then fall down.

The very best houses were built between 1880 and the 1950s when builders tended to put up solid, well-built houses. They were helped by the fact that they didn't have to worry about men in cheap suits carrying clipboards and wearing primrose coloured hard hats telling them that the hardboard walls had to be between 0.01 and 0.011 inches think. Houses built BR ('Before Regulations') were roomier, lighter and better for living in. I don't think it is an exaggeration to say that the more building regulations there are the worse the houses are likely to be. Modern houses and apartment buildings tend to be cold in the winter, hot in the summer, expensive to run, unhealthy, cramped and impractical. Oh, and they have a tendency to catch fire and to burn down very quickly.

Antoinette and I spent a year or two living in a modern house that was around four years old. By the time we moved out, the staircase was coming away from the walls, the windows were falling out of the frames and none of the doors fitted because the walls had moved. We moved for a while to a 16th century house which had a large, modern extension. The 16th century part of the house was as solid as a rock. The modern extension felt temporary.

When I worked as a GP, my patients who lived in Victorian and Edwardian terraced houses were far happier, far more content and far prouder of their homes than the patients who lived in tower blocks or in ticky-tacky box houses on estates. And, of course, those living in terraced houses always had a small garden of their own where they could sit on warm days or grow a few vegetables and flowers of their own. There was a sense of community among people living in terraced houses that never exists among people living in tower blocks – where the lift rarely works, the staircases reek of urine and dog-shit and the sad souls living on the higher floors are often little more than prisoners – or in houses built on a modern, approved estate. Back to back terraced houses were far healthier and better in every way than high rise tower blocks. And far healthier and better in every way than those awful ticky-tacky boxes which builders are forced to build and which usually spring up after the authorities insist on knocking down old, solid, sensible houses which are considered unsuitable for modern living because they have fireplaces and have doorways which aren't wide enough to accommodate a luxury sized two hour luncheon bureaucrat.

Our home (it is much more than a house) is much older than the Bentley, two and a half times older, and it is, I admit, falling apart. But it is falling apart slowly, with style and dignity and grace, and at a gentle pace. And it'll last another century. Or two.

Because the Bentley is so long, I have decided to reverse into our driveway rather than reverse out of it. This is largely to avoid problems with passing pedestrians and dogs rather than passing traffic. (It is more difficult to see out of the back window and the tiny wing mirrors than it is to see out of the windscreen).

Today, we went out for a wonderful drive which went terrifically well except that when we got home I hit one of the stone gate pillars with the rear bumper, putting a very small dent in the chrome. This is yet another piece of evidence that I am an idiot. Our gateway is rather narrow (I think it was built for people who travelled to and fro in a narrow one horse pony cart) and we had agreed that Antoinette would stand in the road and give me hand signals (like a batman directing an aeroplane pilot on an airstrip). She did this perfectly but I am male and males sitting behind steering wheels always dislike taking directions from anyone (it's why male drivers would rather drive around in circles for an hour rather than stop and ask for directions from a stranger). So I hit the gate post. Not very hard, but I hit it.

I've decided that in future I will be more attentive when I watch Antoinette's hands for directions when I'm reversing through the gates. She stands in front of me, keeps an eye on the car and the gate posts and tells me whether I need a little more left hand down a bit or a touch of right hand down a bit.

Only an idiot would find it complicated.

I find it amusing that hydrogen is being sold as the fuel of the future. Those who dislike petrol and diesel cars are very keen on hydrogen. They claim that it is free of pollutants and will, therefore, take us happily into the world of net zero which politicians have promised the global warming cultists. What the proponents do not mention is that hydrogen can only be produced by using fresh water (an increasingly scarce commodity) and some form of fossil fuel. And now the largest global use for natural gas is in the production of hydrogen. You have to laugh, don't you?

I bought a collection of cigarette cards which included a set of cards about Bentley motor cars. I have, over the years, discovered that cigarette cards are a great, quick and (often) fairly cheap way to learn.

I've always collected stuff.

As a boy I collected stamps. In my teenage years I collected beer mats. Then I collected cigarette cards. Most men have at some time in their lives been collectors. Collecting is, I suspect, part of the innate 'hunter-gatherer' gene.

I always found that I learned a great deal from my collection. The beer mats didn't teach me much but the cigarette cards taught me a great deal about history in general and social history in particular. And all of these can be purchased remarkably cheaply. Cigarette cards teach us about the jobs that existed a century or more ago when there were lamp lighters, knocker upperers (employed to bang on bedroom windows to wake people up for work); knife grinders; chair menders; and clock men, employed to go into big houses and wind all the clocks once a week.

More recently I began to collect postcards.

When we lived in Paris we often visited the stamp market (the one which Cary Grant and Audrey Hepburn race through in the film

Charade) and I discovered that there were a number of stalls selling old postcards. And since the cards were incredibly cheap, I often used to buy handfuls of old black and white cards of Paris. I bought some which had been posted and some which were new and unused.

Later, I discovered that there were a number of books dedicated to postcard collecting and that there was even a magazine for collectors. I bought a bundle of old magazines for little more than the price of the postage.

Postcards themselves are also extraordinarily cheap. It is possible to buy a boxful of cards from the late 19th and early 20th century for just a few pounds. And there is certainly no scarcity of cards available. In the early years of the 20th century, post offices around the world dealt with seven billion postcards a year. German publishers produced 36,000 different cards a year. There were series of cards which told a story, cards with tassles, cards which squeaked and cards woven in silk. There were so many cards around that people didn't know what to do with them. Imaginative collectors actually papered their rooms with postcards. In England, printers produced 13 million cards a year depicting cartoons by Donald McGill alone. George Orwell wrote an article about McGill's work in Horizon magazine in September 1941, ending with the words 'I for one should be sorry to see them vanish' and making it clear that he accepted McGill to be one artist rather than a team, as had been rumoured. Two years earlier, Orwell had made the mistake of claiming that the stories in the boys' weekly comics 'Magnet' and 'Germ' could not be the work of the same person. Orwell claimed that no one could possibly write so many stories. In fact they were all written by Charles Harold St John Hamilton who wrote the Magnet stories as Frank Richards, and the Gem stories as Martin Clifford. In addition to writing whole comics by himself, Richards wrote the Greyfriars School books and the Billy Bunter books. His output was prodigious. It has been estimated that he wrote 10,000 words a day for most of his adult life – using an old sit up and beg typewriter. He undoubtedly ended many working days with bleeding fingers. I doubt if even John Creasy or Barbara Cartland produced more published words.

These days, men have stopped collecting stuff and most things which can be collected are now very cheap. Only really rare stamps (such as mint penny blacks) are expensive. Everything else which used to be collected is out of fashion. Boxes of postcards and old magazines can be bought for little more than the cost of the postage. Why? Probably because most adults are too busy playing computer games, updating their Facebook page and watching television.

I picked up a book about classic Bentley motor cars which contained a list of the things which usually go wrong with old cars. The list contained some pretty obvious items: the body, the chrome, the interior, the engine, the gearbox, the chassis and the brakes. Of these it turns out that the most expensive thing to need attention is usually the body work. Buying spare doors, bonnets, and boot lids costs the proverbial arm and a leg. If I'd looked at this book before we'd bought our Bentley, I think I'd have kept the money in the bank.

I started to make a list of things that slowly deteriorate and go wrong with the human body and realised I could sum it all up with one word: everything.

We have a Maserati Ghibli in our driveway. It's a special model, of which they produced just 200, with only a few of them right hand drive. It's a lovely car and it tends to attract admiring glances and comments, particularly from men over the age of 50 who are, I suspect, the last generation to have affection and respect for motor cars as objects to be admired rather than simply used as a way of getting to the shops without getting wet.

But the Maserati is fiendishly, and it seems to me unnecessarily, complicated and, like the computer upon which I am writing this sentence, I understand almost nothing of its potential and, again like the computer, I never use the vast array of extra features with which it is equipped. Indeed, with both car and computer, I find the presence of these extra features more than occasionally disruptive and annoying.

There is a touch screen computer on the Maserati's dashboard, though I don't understand how it works. The satellite navigation system is excellent when I can press the right buttons to turn it on, but the only way I could manage to turn off the radio was to turn on the hands free telephone button. Since I don't have a hands free telephone device, the button simply turned off the radio. This is a useful trick for when the car comes back from a service with the radio blaring away.

And the 91-page quick reference guide to the handbook tells me that I should look out for 62 different little warning lights which will tell me that something is wrong or going wrong.

In addition to all the usual warning signs (a seat belt isn't fastened, the parking brake is on, the oil pressure is low) there are incomprehensive hieroglyphics to tell me that the tyre pressure is low (the car will tell me which tyre has low pressure and precisely what the pressure is for that tyre and all the other tyres); that there is water in the fuel supply; that the headlight aiming system is malfunctioning; that there is ice outside, that the brake pads are becoming worn; that I have exceeded the speed limit; that the AWD is malfunctioning (I don't have the foggiest what that is) and that the AdBlue levels are low (ditto). There are warning lights to tell me that the FCW is malfunctioning, that the LKA is malfunctioning and that the BSA is malfunctioning. Oh and did I mention that there is one to tell me that the AWD is malfunctioning? I did? Oh good. There is a suspension malfunction indicator and an ADAS status indicator which appears only to provide 'examples with only LKA activated and LKA-ACC systems activated'.

And on and on and on it goes – pages and pages of incomprehensible drivel.

I just want to get in the car and drive it. I don't want to have to take a degree in Maserati before I dare sit behind the wheel. Our old Bentley, on the other hand, is simple and straightforward. There is a beautifully contoured knob for the wipers and another for the lights. And if I press a button in the centre of the beautiful dashboard, the petrol gauge (which doesn't work) turns itself into an oil gauge (which does work).

There is tendency to sneer at anything created or built before the start of the 21st century.

But there are many things that used to be done with style and panache that are now done badly or not at all.

Back in Edwardian days, the gent's loo in Leicester Square in central London used to have a plate-glass tank above each urinal. In each tank swam around twenty goldfish. When the flush was released, the water level would sink a couple of inches and the fish would panic for a while. Then, as the tank filled up again, the fish would calm down and carry on swimming. Ben Travers, the playwright, reckoned this was a perfect image of human life as a whole. 'Disaster is about to strike, and then life goes on and we all breathe again.'

It is still quite common to decorate the target area of urinals with small pictures. The aim is to encourage gentlemen visiting the loo to direct their stream more accurately. The urinals at Amsterdam's Schiphol airport have (or had) flies painted on them. In Victorian times the insect to aim at was, for some unknown reason, a bee. Some urinals have mini television screens and visitors can take part in a survey by directing their stream at one or the other. The wall of the gent's loo in a department store in Prague used to be decorated with photos of beautiful, young women all looking downwards. Some of the women looked down approvingly and some looked disappointed.

Today, local authorities are closing public loos as fast as they can. They have a smorgasbord of excuses of which the favourite is: 'We're closing the loos for health and safety reasons'. Second favourite is: 'We're closing the loos because people write on the walls.' Third favourite is: 'Since we closed the loos no one has used them'.

It's really all about money, of course.

Councils now spend a huge proportion of their council tax income to pay the pensions of former employees. There is very little money left for providing services. And so, inevitably, taxes are going to rise and services will continue to diminish. There soon won't be any public loos at all – let alone loos with goldfish on display.

A man in his thirties, taking his dog for a walk, peered over our gate and stood for a moment staring at the Bentley.

'Is that a Rolls Royce?' he asked.

'Close,' I said. 'It's a Bentley S type but it's almost identical to the Rolls Royce Silver Cloud.'

'What year is it?'
'1957.'
'Does it go?'
'It certainly does.'
'Do you keep it outside?'
'We have nowhere else to put it.'
'In the rain and snow?'
I nodded.
'And the sea air?'
'And the sea air,' I agreed.
He shook his head disapprovingly and wandered off.

I understand his point. I'd like to keep the car in a garage but the garage we do have is too small for a car that's nearly 18 feet long. And if we kept a car in the garage where would we keep the mowers, hedge trimmers, leaf blowers and other garden tools? We have space for another garage but we live in an Area of Outstanding Natural Beauty, and the chances of our getting planning permission are slim to very slim to non-existent.

So the car lives outside and will have to put up with the weather. We use it regularly and the only problem I've noticed so far is that the engine takes a couple of moments to start when the weather has been particularly damp. Oh, and the birds seem to use it as target practice which is slightly annoying.

When, over 30 years ago, I had a Bentley S type (and indeed a Silver Cloud of the same vintage) I did have a huge barn. The barn was big enough to store two Bentleys side by side – an S type and a T type – and the cars were molly coddled. I kept a dehumidifier running 24 hours a day and the garage was warm and dry. But I had more trouble starting them than I have with our current S type.

The bottom line is that if I didn't keep the car outside in the open air, I wouldn't be able to have it here at all. And that would sadden me enormously. After all, this is my last glorious misadventure.

However much we admire them and cherish them, the objects which we own are just objects and they have to take their chances and, like the rest of us, put up with the discomforts of life. Our Bentley wasn't bought to exhibit or to take to shows and it wasn't bought as an investment. It was bought to use and enjoy; a constant reminder of a disappearing world. When I'm gone I hope that its next owner will treat it with the same affection.

People have definitely become more intolerant than they used to be – and less willing to accommodate those aspects of life which are part of our social history.

I heard of people who had bought a house a mile away from a classic, long-established motor racing track and then, the minute they'd settled in, made a complaint about the noise and forced the local authority to close the race track.

Didn't they know there was a racetrack there? Of course they did. Didn't they know that racing cars make a noise? Of course they did. Then why do they do what they do? Could it possibly be because they got 20% off the price of their house because of the slight inconvenience caused by the noise of cars racing round a track? And did they know that if they managed to get the motor racing stopped then their new house would automatically increase in value by 20% – allowing them to make a nice profit?

And I read about a church in Beith Ayrshire which has sounded its bell every hour for more than 200 years. The bell has now been silenced after a single noise complaint. The ringing of the bell could only have come as a surprise to the complainant if they had moved to Beith more than 200 years ago.

The really sad thing is that this sort of bizarre occurrence is not rare. It happens every week somewhere.

A farmer in the West Country was prosecuted after his cows attacked a dog walker who had taken his dog with him across one of the farmer's fields. The cows were protective and slightly aggressive because there were calves in the field.

What sort of person is surprised when cows with calves become belligerent under those circumstances?

And what is the farmer to do if he can't put his own cows in his own field?

Theatre managers are so afraid of upsetting their patrons that warnings are given throughout every performance to warn the audience if there is going to be a sudden noise or any outrageous behaviour on the stage. I have no idea what audiences are supposed to do. Cover their eyes and ears perhaps? Walk out and demand a refund?

A church has had to spend a small fortune on dealing with a complaint from a solitary cyclist who objected to spikes on railings outside the church. The railings were protected as of historical value and everyone concerned has been devoting endless amounts of time, and much money, in the search for a way to make the spikes safe for the complaining cyclist.

Just how and why this solitary complainant thought that cyclists might suddenly start flying through the air and impaling themselves on the spikes was not, as far as I know, the subject of any investigation. Why didn't someone in authority have the guts to tell the complainant to go away and boil his head?

It will surely not be long before cyclists demand that roads and all road furniture be made of rubber and that all motorists' vehicles be banned completely.

It is quite extraordinary just how a single individual can cause mayhem within a community. I know of one man in a village who has caused enormous distress to his neighbours. He complained that tiles on a neighbour's roof were reflecting sunlight into his eyes if he sat in a particular position in a specific room in his house. (The trees which stood in between the roof and his eyes were not considered relevant.) Eventually the owner of the roof had to have all his tiles removed and replaced (at his expense) with tiles which were acceptable to the complainant. The complainant then claimed several thousand pounds from the council for the time he had spent making the complaint. The same person also complained when another neighbour had a garden bonfire. There are no laws which prevent people having bonfires to burn garden rubbish but a single complainant from a mischievous moaner can cause the system to purr into action.

We have had our own problems too; with neighbours in a new block of flats complaining that their view of the sea is restricted by a row of trees in our garden. The trees in question are beech trees which have been where they are for considerably longer than the flats have been where they are and, inevitably, far, far longer than the inhabitants of the flats have been where they are. The complainants knew that the trees were there when they purchased their properties but they now want us to cut the trees so that they can have a better view of what is beyond the trees (largely more trees, further away). Several of the flat owners have sent us unpleasant letters and one went so far as to complain to the council in the hope that they could be pressured into forcing us to cut the trees. No one seems to care that the trees are beautiful, that they provide homes for a large amount of wildlife and that they contribute greatly to our privacy.

When I pointed out that the trees lose their leaves in the autumn, and would therefore provide less of an impediment, the main complainant retorted that his flat was a holiday home and that he was only present in it for one month in the summer and that he would not therefore benefit from the absence of leaves.

The Bentley has been rather damp inside recently. We did buy a special cover for £176 but we've never used it after I read somewhere that they can cause problems. We keep the cover, which is huge and very heavy, in the car's boot and there, I suspect, it will stay. The cover is so huge, and heavy, that I fear that if we put it over the car we will probably never take it off. Besides, I like looking at the car and would rather look at the car than the cover.

An Amazon delivery driver stopped his van, peered over our gate and admired the Bentley.

Millennials, and anyone not old enough to be a millennial, thinks that Amazon and Tesco invented home deliveries.

But they didn't, of course.

When I was a boy we had milk delivered daily, and the local corner shop employed a boy with a bicycle who would deliver bread and groceries whenever they were required. We had a telephone, of course, and you could ring up and explain what you wanted. It would be on your kitchen counter within the hour. The paperboy came every morning, including Sunday (and actually put the paper through the letterbox). The postman came twice a day, of course and many of the shops in the nearest town would deliver items that had been purchased. A man came round to mend chairs and another, who travelled on a specially adapted bicycle would sharpen knives or garden equipment. A man with a horse and cart delivered manure 'for your roses, sir' and a rag and bone man clip-clopped past once a week. He'd give housewives a few pence for anything they didn't want – old furniture, pots and pans that needed mending, unwanted clothing, broken lawnmowers and everything else you had that would fit on the back of an always over-laden cart.

Half a century before that there were queues of people delivering all sorts of comestibles and you could have beer or ice delivered by a man with a horse and a trailer.

The main difference now is that today's delivery drivers don't have much time to chat. They are all expected to deliver an extraordinarily high number of letters, packets, parcels or groceries per hour, and I am honestly surprised that most aren't constantly in court accused of speeding. It was a rare moment when the Amazon driver stopped to admire the Bentley.

I have found that Tesco supermarket drivers are mostly extraordinarily well informed, well read and, on the whole, wiser than, say, any sample group of doctors, lawyers, accountants or judges. Conversations maintained in staccato style between fetching crates of groceries from their van have taught me much. Many of the drivers, men in their 40s or 50s, have previously worked in fascinating jobs and have had to take on delivery work because of vicissitudes for which they cannot be held responsible.

One driver told me that he used to work in antiques; buying and selling old English furniture. He began in the antiques business when, while struggling to afford to buy furniture for his first flat, he picked up a 17th century gate leg table and a small linen press for next to nothing. He bought both at a council rubbish dump. At the suggestion of a friend, he put the two items into a furniture auction and made £800 profit. He then became an antique dealer. His business failed for two reasons. First, British builders started building very small houses which weren't big enough to house antique furniture (particularly the once popular, solidly made 'brown furniture' that was so popular in Victorian times). Second, American dealers stopped flying to Britain in the aftermath of the 9/11 attacks in New York. Prior to that date, American dealers had bought up everything they could find and shipped it back to the United States. But after the American dealers stopped coming over, prices fell dramatically and never recovered.

While writing this book, I have tried hard not to look at the past uncritically; falsely imagining that everything then was much better than it is now. Driving a car which is 67-years-old it would be an easy trap to fall into.

I'm well aware that there must be some things that are better today than they were 50, 60 or 70 years ago and I'm quite sure that if I keep concentrating I will eventually think of them.

But, try as I might, I cannot convince myself that workmen today are better, in any respect, than workmen half a century ago.

The garage which is looking after the Bentley seems to be run and staffed by honest and decent people who are content to provide a decent service for a fair price; this is just as well because there are few suitable garages left in the country which can look after old cars. The number of garages has presumably fallen as the number of classic cars has dropped.

This is a huge relief because my experience of workmen in recent years has not been a good one. We have, in the last couple of decades, employed a good many builders and the only thing I can say with confidence is that the quality of the work done and the integrity of the workmen themselves has fallen steadily and rapidly.

I have found it nigh on impossible to find workmen who are prepared to do an honest day's work for an honest day's pay. Workmen who come to the house insist on having their radio playing all day long (whether they are working inside or outside) and several have insisted on bringing their dogs with them. One carpenter brought two dogs which never stopped barking, which were so unfriendly that neither Antoinette nor I dared go out into the garden where they were running loose and which left the lawn and the rest of the garden in a mess. Worse still, they chased the birds and squirrels who are regular visitors to the garden. They (the workmen not their dogs) spend their days hunched over their smart phones and if you approach them quietly, when they are supposed to be working, will invariably be scrolling through their emails and texts. 'I'm just checking on the availability of parts,' they'll tell you with a straight face when they're supposed to be fitting a new tap. At regular intervals throughout the day they'll be found sitting in their van, eating, drinking and looking at their phones. And, of course, they constantly require cups of tea or coffee, usually requiring something far more complicated than just a cup of tea. ('Don't you have Darjeeling? I thought you'd have Darjeeling.') They never listen when you tell them what you want them to do and they never, ever write down any of the instructions you give them. (Watch 'Mr Blandings Builds his Dream House' starring Cary Grant and Myrna Loy.)

Workmen promise to turn up and then disappear completely. They start work, leave the house in a mess and then disappear for days at a time. They say they will arrive at 8.00 am sharp and so I get up at 7.00, open the front gate and then sit and wait and fume until they turn up at 3 pm and stay for just long enough to unload some stuff which they dump in the most inconvenient position possible. They turn on their portable radio the moment they arrive and leave it playing until they leave. They do poor work and charge top rate prices. They produce quotes and estimates which bear no resemblance to the final bill. (There are always reasons for the discrepancies and I know now that the words 'quote' and 'estimate' are merely tokens in a one-sided negotiation process.)

When workmen do turn up they are too often rude and careless. One heating engineer arrived and immediately dropped his heavy tool box onto my shoes and then looked at me and smirked. An electrician had, within thirty minutes, knocked over the refrigerator and split a floorboard that he was lifting. Irritated by a pile of books which he had decided were in his way, he picked them up and threw them across the room. Neither he nor his boss could understand why I threw him out of the house.

When they do deign to arrive, they make a mess, dig a hole, break something and then disappear for half a day (allegedly to fetch materials) or a week (allegedly to deal with an emergency somewhere else). When they go to fetch materials it's on your time, of course, and even if the building supplies store is only five minutes away, it always takes them half a day to get there, buy what they need and return.

If, after they've gone for a week, you ring them or email they become upset and hurt. 'You'd want me to deal with your emergency straight away, wouldn't you?'

For every hour that they work they spend two hours playing with their mobile phone, updating their Facebook page, adding photos to their Instagram page and dealing with their emails. And they always want to show you their boring photos. They have photos of their boat, their holiday home, their family, their in-laws and their recent three week holiday in Barbados.

And most of them are precious, spoilt and entitled.

Our front door is always kept locked and bolted and covered with a huge draught excluder and a very thick curtain. This isn't just for security, it's because the front door is actually two doors and there are gaps wide enough for mice to walk through hand in hand. The thick curtain is there to keep out the north easterly winds which can otherwise double our heating bill. We opened the doors when we moved into the house and had large, heavy furniture delivered. But for many years now the doors have remained locked, bolted, barred and curtained.

And so when workmen come we let them into the house through the back door. It's the door we use ourselves. It's the door everyone uses. But today's workmen don't like entering a house through the back door. Twice recently I've had to apologise profusely to workmen who were deeply offended because they were expected to enter that way.

'You want me to come through the tradesman's entrance, eh?' they sniff, clearly regarding it as a slight; an example of typical, 19th century Victorian social elitism.

Once they're in I used to nervously ask workmen if they would be kind enough to remove their shoes before wandering around the house.

A long time ago that always worked. Actually, they usually didn't need asking. These days I wouldn't dare say a word.

'I have to wear these all the time,' snapped a plumber once, pointing to his footwear. 'In case I drop something on my feet.' He was wearing dirty plimsolls and was wandering around the house checking radiators. He was carrying no tools.

'I'm wearing safety shoes,' said a carpet fitter. 'It's against the law for me to take them off.'

We bought a supply of slip on plastic shoe covers and we do offer these. They usually put them on as a huge favour and they puff and huff and make an enormous fuss about it. And warn us that if they slip and fall because they're wearing our plastic shoe covers then we will be responsible. Too many seem to think it is their right to traipse mud around the whole house.

Workmen expect endless cups of tea, they need to use the loo every thirty minutes (and stay in there for twenty minutes at a time) and even if they're working outside they turn up their noses at using the gardener's loo, which is neat and smart but outside the main house. We put out platefuls of wrapped chocolate biscuits for them to munch, and the plate is always empty when they leave. They can't have possibly eaten them all and must pour the plateful of goodies into their pockets or tool bag.

And in winter, they always leave the doors open.

In the middle of winter a workman came to put in yet another new boiler.

I settled him in the boiler room, warned him not to leave the back door open because if he did the house would be full of inquisitive squirrels, and left him there for an hour and a half or so.

I then suddenly started to shiver.

Even though he knew we were struggling to keep the house tolerably warm with a pile of electric heaters, he had disappeared and left the back door as wide open as it would go. Outside, the temperature was around freezing and the inside temperature was, inevitably, dropping fast.

I eventually found him sitting in the warm of his van drinking hot tea from a flask.

I shouted at him I'm afraid, and I didn't feel bad about it afterwards. I found out later that the moment I'd left him he'd telephoned his boss to complain about me.

It took me around six hours to get warm again afterwards. When you get older the cold seems to get into the bones and it is difficult to warm them up.

Some people are allergic to pollen. Some are allergic to nuts. I'm definitely allergic to workmen. They always seem to bring me out in a red-faced, expletive laden fury.

Idiots from a plumbing company connected a bathroom radiator to the hot water system instead of the central heating system and so the radiator only gets hot when a hot water tap is opened. Moreover, the two systems are connected in some strange way which now means that every morning I have to refill the heating system with more water.

The other day we had a workman in the house who spent three hours fixing three brackets in a bathroom. The brackets were to hold up a shower curtain. The final price to provide the brackets and to fit them to the wall was just over £500, and the workmen spent more time looking at his smart phone than he spent fixing the brackets.

It was this experience which made me realise that I could probably do just as good a job myself, and free myself from the tyranny of workmen. I could do it more speedily and with less fuss. And I could do it a lot cheaper. And what was the downside? Most of the workmen we've hired recently have done shoddy work. I was pretty confident that I could do shoddy work at a more competitive price than any professional. And when I have finished the job I will clear up after myself.

When I first owned property I never bothered to try to do any DIY jobs myself. It was easier, quicker and cheaper to hire a professional. There were always carpenters, plumbers, electricians, roofers and odd job men around who were happy to turn up with a bag of tools and do an honest day's work for a fair day's pay. They were reliable, conscientious and they knew what they were doing. They didn't have certificates and diplomas but they could do things that needed doing without sitting in their van and watching a YouTube video.

Everything has changed and most of today's workmen are demanding, lazy, incompetent and rude.

I decided to do a little gentle 'do it yourself'.

It's not as if I am a complete neophyte. Many years ago I wrote an article for 'Do It Yourself' magazine. (I can't remember what it was about and I don't have a copy.) And I wrote an article for 'The Lady' magazine on how best to hang pictures on the wall alongside a staircase. (My advice, in case you are interested, was to stand on each stair in turn. Press your nose against the wall and make a small cross with a pencil at that point. Bang in nail. Hang picture.)

To begin with, I bought myself a few essential tools and something called a 'Workmate'.

I thought it would come assembled but it wasn't. It was a nightmare. My idea of 'it comes ready assembled' is taking it out of the box and being able to use it. Socks are assembled and ready to use. But my Workmate definitely wasn't assembled. It was like buying a pair of shoes and getting a box which contained the soles, the uppers, the heels, the tongue and some shoe laces and being expected to get on with it.

I then set to work mending a rotten windowsill and an equally rotten fascia board.

When I'd finished, I bought a pot of yacht varnish and a pack of ridiculously cheap paintbrushes. I then painted the (very sticky) yacht varnish over the new wood. I reckoned that if anything was going to be waterproof it would be yacht varnish. The brush I used did its job perfectly adequately, and I dealt with the problem of cleaning it afterwards by tossing it into the bag of rubbish I keep for the bonfire.

I'm getting better at it.

I dug out rotten wood and fixed bits of new wood on top of the rotten stuff to keep out rain and rodents. I even managed to fix a draught excluder to the bottom of an outside door at exactly the right level. I fitted barriers to a bird table to stop nuts falling over the edge.

Not having to deal with workmen is a joy.

We went out for a ride in the Bentley today and it started to rain. The windscreen wipers are small and work quite well but they are unsynchronised. They stutter a little, as though they are not quite sure what to do, and they look as though they might eventually bump into each other, though I am sure they won't. It was clearly an effort for them to move from one side of the windscreen to the other, and I was reminded of myself climbing a steep hill or a long flight of stairs. I drove slowly to give the wipers time to move the raindrops out of the way. I don't think I've ever felt sorry for inanimate objects before but I felt sorry for these wipers as they struggled to do their duty.

I must confess, though, that the struggling wipers look wonderfully charming in a strange way. I think we need two new wiper blades and when I have worked out how to fit them, we can just buy the rubber bits to fit into the metal blades. Actually, our new old Bentley and our old new Maserati both need new windscreen wipers. I can buy new blades to fit onto the Bentley's wipers. They cost just a few shillings. But for the Maserati I must purchase a pair of complete new wipers (not just the blades) for £70.

Since the headlights aren't as powerful as those on modern cars, we have decided to avoid going out in the Bentley in the dark or the rain but particularly when it is both dark and raining.

I tend to drive slowly when we are in the Bentley which has no seat belts, padded dashboard or airbags and the windscreen glass isn't the sort that is fitted these days (we could, I have no doubt, have all these things fitted but it would be like a ballet dancer wearing basketball shoes with a tutu). I usually cruise at between 30 mph and 50 mph where there is no speed limit although the old lady still moves with considerable speed when I put my foot down, and I suspect she'd still get somewhere near to 100 mph if I wanted her to do so. But the car and I are both past our speeding days, and as someone who has for decades rushed hither and thither, I must admit that pootling along, while settled on a comfortable, soft sofa, seems very pleasant.

Seat belts have been compulsory in the UK for some while but were first introduced in the 1960s in the USA when it was compulsory for cars to be fitted with seat belts and padded dashboards. The aim, of course, was to improve road safety and, as intended, there were fewer road deaths per accident. But because cars were safer, people drove more recklessly and had more accidents. The end result was that having seat belts made no damned difference.

This isn't the only instance of a law backfiring, changing behaviour and ending up doing no good. When the window tax was introduced in England, owners of large houses bricked up lots of windows so that they paid less tax. The end result was that the Government was no better off and people lived in the dark. In the 1990s, around a dozen European countries introduced wealth taxes. Most of them gave up when people either left the country or just worked less. In France the wealth tax brought in only half of the tax that was lost because people were emigrating. Rent controls always have a negative effect too. Rent controls which limit the prices landlords can charge for property result in landlords giving up being landlords. And the result of that is a shortage of properties to rent. And the result of that is that rents go up. Nothing changes and politicians never learn.

Once you start looking for daft laws it seems that there are no end of them. In 1712, England imposed a tax on printed wallpaper. Folk got round the tax by putting up plain paper and then painting patterns onto the paper. In 1784, a tax on hats was introduced. Hat makers got round this by calling their products 'headgear'. It took the authorities 20 years to respond by taxing 'headgear'. There have been equally potty laws in America. In Rumford, Maine, it was illegal for a tenant to bite a landlord. In Youngstown, Ohio, it was illegal to tie a giraffe to a lamppost. In Nogales, Arizona, men could get into trouble if they wore braces. In San Francisco, it was illegal to shoot jack rabbits from a cable car. In Owensboro, Kentucky, a woman could be arrested for buying a new hat unless her husband had tried it on first. In Carmel, California, it was illegal to take a bath in a business office. In Norton, Virginia, it was illegal for a man to tickle a girl. Quite right too, you might say.

We laugh at these crazy laws. But today's laws are ever pottier. In Canada it is illegal to use the words 'boy' and 'girl' since they are considered right wing and dangerous and in the UK, it is considered racist to teach or learn mathematics.

Once every couple of weeks, Antoinette and I go out for an afternoon spin in the countryside, and our generally aimless trips remind me of the days in the 1950s when I was a boy and most families who had motor cars went for a Sunday afternoon drive. (It doesn't actually have to be on a Sunday afternoon, of course. But such trips were always known as 'Sunday afternoon drives'). My parents used to take a relative or two for a drive. Occasionally, we would take a picnic and find a suitable field somewhere. Sometimes we'd stop off at a café and have a cream tea. But the journey was the true destination. Petrol was three shillings and sixpence a gallon in old money, and I remember the shock when it went up to three shillings and ninepence.

Driving slowly through the countryside means that you see far more of whatever there is to see, of course. And rather to my surprise, we never get tooted. Maybe the motorists behind us absorb the pootling feeling. Maybe they find that they too are happy to drive along slowly. Or perhaps they don't think it would be right to toot and try to hurry up a dowager on an excursion. Frequently a driver will wave cheerily as they pass. One day a fellow on an old motorbike roared past and held a thumb high in the air in appreciation. I gave him a couple of dignified toots on the horn in appreciation.

I have absolutely no doubt that our old Bentley gives other motorists a great deal of passing pleasure.

It is astonishing just how easily we have adapted to a world in which we accept that anything 'new' must be better than anything 'old'.

I'm writing this book on what used to be called a word processor. It's actually a laptop but it isn't connected to the internet. To avoid back and neck ache, I sit the laptop on a pile of thick books and type using a separate, old-fashioned keyboard which is connected to the laptop by a bit of wire. The keyboard is much better to use than the keyboard on the laptop which I find virtually impossible to operate with anything resembling success.

I have in my life used a wide variety of machines. I started, of course, with an old-fashioned sit up and beg typewriter, something which Mark Twain would have recognised, and worked my way through an Olympia, an Olivetti and an IBM golf-ball machine.

Nothing has ever worked as well or as efficiently as the old-fashioned Olympia. It was a little smoother to use than my old sit up and beg machine, which had to be pounded to put any ink onto the paper. I used to type out my notes and then spread all the sheets of paper onto a flat surface (I found a snooker table was perfect) and use scissors to cut up the various sections. I could then staple or Sellotape the sections onto fresh sheets of paper before retyping each section. To anyone under 50, this probably sounds fiendishly onerous but it worked incredibly well, and it was faster and more efficient than trying to switch between different screens on a computer. When I'd finished a chapter, I would photocopy it on an old flat-bed copier and put the copy into a metal box in a barn.

The individuals who invented the computer, and then turned a machine based mathematician into a convenient, portable tool, are widely feted and honoured. They should not be. The computer has steadily destroyed almost everything we used to value.

And then the British establishment gave Tim Berners-Lee a knighthood for his part in inventing the internet. That too was a huge mistake. They should have given Mr Berners-Lee 30 years hard labour and made him return the key to hell to the devil. The internet has done more to damage humanity than Hitler, Genghis Khan and Attila the Hun combined. The internet has permanently changed history, it has replaced the history books, it has demolished truth and side-lined honour and integrity and it will gradually destroy everything which we had learned to value.

It isn't generally realised just how much electricity is used by computers and data centres. In fact data centres consume a huge proportion of any nation's electricity. In Ireland, for example, data centres consume 18% of the nation's available electricity. It is ironic that much of that electricity, derived largely from fossil fuels, is used by climate change campaigners sending each other emails bemoaning the approaching end of the world and calling for an end to the use of fossil fuels.

A fellow I don't know but who walks his dog past our gate twice a day stopped and stared at our Bentley yesterday. I happened to be nearby cutting back some bushes which had grown into a space I wanted for other purposes.

'Bit old, that, isn't it?' he said, with something of a sneer. 'Rolls Royce is it?'

It still surprises me that many people can't tell a Bentley from a Rolls Royce.

'I suspect it's younger than both of us. It was born in 1957,' I told him. 'And it's a Bentley.'

'Looks like a Rolls Royce,' he said. 'Are you sure it isn't a Rolls Royce? I can tell them by the radiator.' His dog, which clearly wasn't very bright, mistook one of our gateposts for a lamppost. Or maybe he thought it was a tree.

'I'm sure,' I said. 'The only difference between a Rolls Royce and a Bentley is the radiator – and the hood ornament.'

He sniffed, shook his head and glowered. 'You'd be better off with a little electric car,' he said. 'I've got one.' He nodded towards the Bentley. 'Bit barking having one of those,' he said. 'Bit eccentric.' He took one last look. 'I think you'll find it's a Rolls Royce,' he added. 'I know cars.'

He called his dog and they moved off.

Is owning a 67-year-old car (and using it regularly) an eccentric thing to do? It doesn't seem eccentric though I realise that one definition of eccentricity might be to behave in what others think is an unusual way but to consider your behaviour to be quite normal.

Heigh ho.

Frankly, my dear, I don't give a damn.

As I believe that someone once said.

Some of my favourite people are eccentrics, though only the natural ones (such as Fred Basson, possibly the world's most enthusiastic collector of cigarette cards) are appealing. I have written a good deal in the past about great eccentrics (truly magnificent ones such as John Mytton were ten a penny in the days before telephones, radio, televisions and motor cars) but in recent years true eccentrics have been replaced by exhibitionists with publicity agents and managers who carefully manufacture fake personalities for their clients. These sorry souls are eager to promote themselves on social media so that they can become influencers and sell over-priced and useless products to the gullible millions.

I like reading about eccentric events too. For example, how about the 37 course lunch which was held on November 17th of 2003? The meal was based on recipes by great cooks and food writers and drawn from cookbooks published between 1654 and 1823 and the food was accompanied by 13 wines. I'd have been sick for a month if I'd eaten a quarter of the courses. But for these brave gourmands, life is a near-death experience and they were determined to push themselves to the limit. A cook, his wife and 39 cooks and waiters were responsible for preparing and serving the meals.

'If I announced that I and eleven other diners shared a 37 course lunch that likely cost as much as a new Volvo station wagon,' wrote Jim Harrison, one of the diners, 'those of a critical nature will let their minds run in tiny, aghast circles of condemnation. My response to them is that none of us twelve disciples of gourmandise wanted a new Volvo. We wanted only lunch, and since lunch lasted approximately eleven hours, we saved money by not having to buy dinner.'

That's eccentric.

For the third time in a week someone told me that I should drive an electric car.

Electric cars are a confidence trick being played upon a gullible and susceptible public. The folk who bought them enjoyed grants, tax deals, cheaper road taxes and free travel in cities, but they soon found that the financial disadvantages far outweigh the advantages.

For example, drivers are paying 27% more to insure an electric car than they would pay to insure a petrol or diesel version of the same vehicle. The reason is simple: electric cars are more complex than cars with internal combustion engines and when they go wrong they cost more to put right.

And, of course, electric cars have a much shorter life span than cars which rely on petrol or diesel. The batteries used in electric cars die after a few years and the cost of replacing them is so high that it's cheaper to scrap the car and buy another one. Since it has been proved that it takes more energy to build an electric car than a proper car it is clear that the short life of an electric car means that it is really bad for the environment. (Producing electricity to keep an electric car moving puts a huge strain on electric supplies, and since most electricity is produced by burning fossil fuels of one sort or another, it is clear that the whole process is an extraordinarily expensive and pointless exercise in hypocrisy and futility.)

Early in 2024, it was revealed that the alleged mileage range achieved by electric cars has been dramatically over-estimated. One major survey suggested that electric cars travel around 18% fewer miles than their manufacturers promise. It is known too that electric cars manage far fewer miles on a charge if the weather isn't quite right. And the driver who goes at more than 28 mph will find his battery packing up rather speedily. And then, of course, he'll probably find that he is many miles away from a charging point.

Electric vehicles have been around for much longer than most people realise, and were first abandoned a century ago when it was found that, for a number of reasons, vehicles driven by petrol were infinitely superior in every way. This truth has been rediscovered and large companies which had fallen for the idea that electric cars were the way forward, have now changed their minds. For example,

Hertz the car hire company has announced that it is selling a third of its fleet of electric vehicles and replacing them with petrol driven models. Other companies are doing the same.

All this means that while governments everywhere are pouring billions of pounds of taxpayers' money into subsidies for electric cars, consumers aren't buying them. Motorists prefer to have a car which they can fill with fuel when they need to, instead of worrying that their batteries are going to let them down 100 miles from home without a working charger in sight.

No one, it seems, wins out of the obsession with electric cars. Even car manufacturers are losing out. Ford is said to be losing $36,000 on every electric car it sells. There is a global shortage of minerals required to build electric vehicles, and in those countries where the essential minerals can be found, small children are employed to dig from morning to night.

Since it has been proved beyond doubt that it takes more energy to build an electric car than a proper car (with an internal combustion engine fed with petrol or diesel) and that a petrol or diesel driven car is infinitely better for the environment, the raison d'etre for electric cars is non-existent. Additionally, it is clear that the short life of an electric car means that it is really bad for the environment.

It is also worth noting that since electric cars are more or less silent, they are known as 'quiet killers'. A high proportion of serious road traffic accidents are caused by electric cars. Pedestrians would be much better off if, instead of introducing absurd 20 mph speed limits, local politicians introduced a ban on electric vehicles (with the possible exception of speed restricted milk floats if there are any left in service).

Motorists who want a more interesting motor car would do better to buy a classic car – built in the days when cars were built to last and had character.

I can recommend a Bentley S type motor car. There are a few of them left.

As I edge cautiously towards another birthday, I am pleased to say that I don't feel a day over 77.

I know several people in their 70s and 80s who refuse to go to the optician for an eye test because they are worried that if the optician finds something vaguely wrong with their eyes then he or she will be duty bound to report them to the Authorities and they will lose their driving licence. With no public transport in many parts of the country, a driving licence is essential. For the same reason many older folk refuse to talk about eye problems to their GP.

A former neighbour, who now lives 100 miles away, went to see an optician for a routine test. The optician decided that their patient had a serious eye problem and told them that they could not drive home. He also wrote to the Driver and Vehicle Licensing Authority (DVLA) to report his advice. The neighbour was too scared to drive his car home and had to get a taxi. He then had to pay a local garage to retrieve his car from the car park where he had left it. The cost of this service, the extra parking charge and the penalty cost him over £250. The DVLA wrote and told him that he could no longer drive his car. Since his wife did not drive and there was no bus service in their area, they were marooned in their home. (Local councils in the UK have cut over 90% of all bus services since 2010. Thousands of country dwellers who don't have cars are being forced to abandon their gardens and their animals and to move into tiny, cardboard-walled flats in the developing 20 minute cities.) The nearest taxi service was 20 miles away and so busy that they required two weeks' notice.

Two months later, a consultant ophthalmologist reported that our neighbour did not have an eye problem. The optician's diagnosis had been wrong. But the DVLA would not give our neighbour his licence back and told him that he would have to take a fresh driving test. After a lifetime of blameless driving, he couldn't face the idea and so he and his wife were forced to move into a flat in a nearby town. It is no exaggeration to say that their lives are ruined.

The war on motorists, cars and travel is hotting up. The European Union (which seems to hate poor people) is apparently proposing to ban repairs on all cars which are more than 15-years-old. This new ban will clearly have a serious effect on people who drive old cars. It will very much affect tradesmen who use old vans, and country dwellers who cannot afford a new (or even fairly new) car but who need transport if they are to get to the shops or take the children to school.

The plan is to ban repair work on faults which affect the engine, the brakes, the gearbox, the chassis, the steering or the bodywork. Presumably, faults which affect the radio, the tyres and the windscreen wipers will be allowed. This attack on those who cannot afford shiny new cars will, of course, also destroy many garages and put huge numbers of mechanics out of work. Companies manufacturing parts for motor cars will also be left high and dry. The new legislation is wasteful and bad for the environment in every conceivable respect. It is pointless and appears both spiteful and elitist.

Theoretically, the UK isn't in the EU anymore since the electorate wisely chose to leave the world's first combined communist and fascist state back in 2016. But the British Government has consistently ignored the wishes of the people and has adopted pretty well all of the EU's oppressive, dictatorial legislation, and I have little doubt that they'll adopt this new law too.

And, by one of those curious modern coincidences that clearly aren't coincidences, similarly bits of legislation are already being passed in America.

I wonder how this proposed legislation will affect classic, vintage and veteran motor cars. Technically, I suppose that the law will mean that it will be illegal and impossible for anyone to repair our Bentley. And the legislation will mean that the roads will be full of tiny, tinny, expensive, dangerous and pretty well useless electric cars.

The comforting thought is that the people who own and run classic cars are a feisty bunch and won't take this lying down. If the proposed legislation goes through, there will, I suspect, be an exception made for really old cars (which already have special rights to travel in cities where there are restrictions and fees for cars which aren't run on electricity).

If the legislation isn't changed then a black market will doubtless spring up and we'll have to take the Bentley to a lock up garage somewhere and find a mechanic prepared to continue looking after an elderly lady. One thing is for sure: if keeping our Bentley alive means breaking the law then the law will just have to put up with being broken.

The Bentley struggled a little going up a hill today. We sat, patiently, and eventually it reached the top of the hill without any real problem. I feel much sympathy for it.

I find that I can do less than I could do a year ago before becoming tired. If I spend half an hour working in the garden I have to rest for a while. If I go for a walk I welcome benches along the way. Not surprisingly, the older I get and the slower I become, the more respect I have for time. When I was young I had very little respect for time; there seemed to be endless supplies of it and so I squandered it without a thought or a care in the world. Now that my supplies are clearly limited, I cherish each day and each hour and I resent anyone or anything which wastes my time. I have always been impatient but these days I have less patience than ever.

Other things are happening too.

I find that although I have a tendency to forget things (if I go into the garage to do half a dozen things I have to write them down or else I'll forget one of them) my mind is full of memories from my childhood and my years at medical school. We are, I suppose, built on and out of our memories. (Writing things down has always seemed a sensible idea. I am tired of workmen who never write anything down and then forget half the things they're supposed to do.)

Still, my understanding of my ignorance grows daily with age.

It's what we don't know that we don't know which is vital, of course.

By the time we reach our teenage year, we feel we know everything we need to know and our confidence grows rapidly. By the ripe old age of 15 years we know everything there is to know.

Humans used to stay at this peak 'knowing' position until they reached their early twenties and then slowly but remorselessly they would lose their confidence and gain in ignorance, and gradually learn to acknowledge their ignorance. The more they saw, the more they learnt, the more they realised just how much they didn't know. And that ignorance increased as the years went by. By the time they reached their biblically allotted three score years and ten, they had acquired knowledge and experience and were almost embarrassed by the extent of their ignorance.

Sadly, all that has changed.

Millennials and the Z generation never grow out of their feeling of omniscience and are not interested in taking advice from their older friends, relatives or colleagues.

They prefer to be fed ready-made opinions, conclusions and advice, preferably from their favourite internet apps, rather than to be expected to think and value information themselves.

When, why and how, I wonder, did mankind choose to reject experience and wisdom?

I have owned and driven modern Bentleys and I've owned and driven old ones and there is absolutely no doubt in my mind that the old ones are better. Modern motor cars are far too complex for their own good. All the electrical equipment with which they are fitted means that modern, sophisticated cars have to be connected up to the mains every two weeks or so in order to keep their batteries alive. Go away for three weeks and come back to your car in the airport or station car park and you'll probably have to ring for assistance.

Our Bentley S type is a perfect example of the time when engineers reached the peak of perfection. The car has an automatic gear box (which is massively useful but which can be overridden if an extra burst of power is required), power steering (definitely useful) and two speed windscreen wipers (useful when the weather is bad) but the designers didn't lose touch with reality.

For example, there is a button on the dashboard which, when pressed, releases the cover over the entrance to the petrol tank. In the far off days when garages were staffed by human beings who put the petrol into the tank, took the driver's money and, if required, wiped the windscreen and checked the oil and water, this was a handy device. It meant that the driver could choose whether or not to stretch his legs. If the weather was inclement he could stay in the car. If the weather was good he could take a small stroll around the garage forecourt while the attendant filled the tank. The fuel would, of course, be paid for with cash.

But, and this is the brilliant bit, the car's designers were well aware of the risk that if the button to open the petrol tank cover didn't work then the driver would be in a pickle. And so, inside the boot (which is opened by an ordinary old-fashioned key), and easily reachable even if the boot is full of luggage, there is a small loop of wire. Pull on the wire loop and the petrol cap cover flips open.

I reckon that the invention and installation of that loop of wire marked the point at which progress in the business of building motor cars reached the end.

Since then, I'm afraid that far too many people have mistaken change for progress.

It's difficult to decide just when progress went too far.

Was it the indefinite day when charabancs became known as coaches and were fitted with loos and tea making equipment so that stops at sometimes pleasant and always fascinating wayside hostelries were no longer necessary?

Was it when AA men gave up their three wheeled motorcycles and stopped saluting vehicles which had an AA membership badge fixed to the radiator or front bumper?

Was it when the authorities started to tell manufacturers how to design their cars so that they met bureaucratic rules which they had decided were more important than aesthetics?

Was it when motorists stopped taking elderly relatives out for a Sunday drive and a cream tea at Ye Olde Tea Shoppe down a country lane just three miles off the by-pass?

Was it when motorways were first introduced, making it possible for road menders to create 40 mile tailbacks of traffic?

Maybe.

But I suspect that things first went wrong with the world when every home was given a zip code or a postcode. That was the moment when the world was prepared for computers to take over. We were told that was progress. But ever since postcodes were introduced, the quality of the mail service has gone downhill.

In Victorian times, the postman delivered mail four to six times a day and still had time to stop and talk, to carry messages and to take away packets and parcels for posting. This meant that if a housewife was planning her evening meal, she could write to the butcher and the greengrocer asking if they had good lamb chops or some good sausages available. Within hours she would have her reply. She could then write back with her order. And the comestibles would be delivered in good time for dinner to be prepared. Today, you're lucky if a letter posted today arrives at its destination within a week. We marvel at Amazon's ability to deliver within 24 hours but all they've really done is to take us back to Victorian days.

Fifty to a hundred years ago people used to entertain themselves. People went to concerts or the theatre or the circus or organised singing around the piano in the pub or someone's home. Then came the cinema, then the radio, then the television and now social media has created toxic isolation.

I'm sure you can remember when dustbins were collected and emptied once a week (without home owners having to touch them or spend hours washing out their yoghurt cartons and sorting their cardboard).

Not all that long ago there were regular local bus services and before a man called Beeching came along, a network of small local railway stations connected small towns and villages with major cities everywhere.

The self-employed and those running small businesses struggle daily with bureaucracy and despair. Villages have lost their shops and their pubs and their schools. Towns have lost their banks, their post offices and their cinemas. The absence of banks means it is hardly surprising that four out of ten people now never use cash at all (presumably without knowing or caring that in eschewing cash they are part of the new world of digitalisation and social credit.) I can take you to decent sized towns where it is difficult to buy a postage stamp, a newspaper or a magazine and where it is impossible to have a shoe repaired or a key cut. If you want a plumber you have to go online, and misleading adverts will mean that you'll probably end up with a tradesman who has to drive 50 or 100 miles to reach you, and charge accordingly.

Public libraries were open for long hours and mobile library services supplied the housebound.

Most people didn't own as many clothes then as they do today, but the clothes they had were infinitely better made and lasted much longer. I have a jacket, trousers and a jumper which I bought half a century ago and they still look and feel good. Even books were better made then than they are now.

Vicars now look after churches spread across half a dozen

villages (or more) and have no time or inclination (or sense of service) to visit the elderly, the lonely or the infirm. The sense of community has gone, replaced by the sense of entitlement and an obsession with 'work-life' balance. Today, people in cities, towns and villages die alone and are not missed until someone notices that the mailbox is overflowing with circulars and junk mail.

Museums and art galleries were open to all and there were no bullet-proof glass screens in front of famous paintings. Visitors could stand inches from La Pieta and the Venus de Milo and admire the Mona Lisa and The Nightwatch without a thick protective screen being necessary (and without the fear that insane campaigners might appear at any moment and throw paint or soup at the picture for some unfathomable reason).

Everywhere we look now there are signs that we have travelled too far along the road towards technical perfection and away from a civilised way of living.

When was life at its best?

A long time ago, that's for sure.

Mental illness is commoner than ever (and not just because it is more recognised now than before) and a scarily high percentage of the population regularly take, and depend on, anxiolytics, antidepressants, sleeping tablets and other psychotropic drugs. Millions of people are hooked on drugs which do them no good whatsoever, and which do them a great deal of harm. Loneliness is endemic in cities, towns, villages and the countryside. Doctors work in huge health centres, and patients rarely see the same doctor twice. Cottage hospitals have been closed as have village halls.

I have spent most of my life writing about medicine and health care, and a couple of years ago I decided, quite seriously, that health care in Britain in the third decade of the 21st century was worse than it had been half a century earlier.

I was, I repeat, deadly serious about this. And the facts prove that I am right. The quality of health is poorer than it was 50 years ago. Life expectation is falling. There have been very few useful new drugs or procedures introduced in the last 50 years – and none of them has made a dramatic difference to the majority of patients. Survival rates for patients suffering from serious disorders are falling. Waiting lists to see a GP or a hospital consultant are longer than ever before. Waiting times for an ambulance are longer than ever. The number of patients being killed by doctors and nurses is higher than ever. The incidence of serious side effects is higher than ever. And so on and so on.

However, when I examined the evidence closely, I came to the conclusion that I was wrong in claiming that health care had been better 50 years earlier. In fact, health care was better 75 years ago, not just 50 years ago.

Three quarters of a century ago, patients who fell ill at night, during a weekend or on a bank holiday could pick up the telephone and expect to be visited at home by a family doctor whom they knew and who knew them.

Today, a patient who falls ill at night, during a weekend or on a bank holiday has to ring for an ambulance and hope that one arrives within 48 hours or they have to make their own way to the local Accident and Emergency Unit of their nearest hospital (which may be 30 to 50 miles away) and hope that they are seen (probably by a nurse) within 24 hours.

GPs won't even visit their patients during the day time. Patients wishing to report emergency problems are told (by a machine) to call an ambulance. Now that calling an ambulance may mean a two or three day wait, the advice might as well be 'call the undertaker'.

There is no doubt that the quality of caring was infinitely better in the 1950s than it is today. Today no one in the medical establishment is much interested in patient care or in truth and respect – these things are expensive to provide, they are inconvenient for the system and they do not fit the Agenda. There is today little or no understanding of the importance of holistic medicine, of the healing power of the body, of the effect of the placebo and so on.

Hospitals used to be run with the patients in mind. Today, hospitals are run by bureaucrats for the sake of the staff. The patients are an afterthought; an inconvenience. Doctors and nurses have no understanding of the relationship between the mind and the body. The widespread, modern assumption that people are all the same is as false as the assumption that grains of sand are identical (they aren't) or that snowflakes are identical (they aren't). Medicine has failed because of the drive deeper and deeper into specialisation and further and further away from the treatment of the individual. And it has failed because nurses have been told that they should consider themselves too important for simple caring. The modern nurse is taught to regard herself as a faux doctor.

I recently watched a magnificent film called 'Monte Walsh' which tells the story of the last cowboy, a man holding onto a way of life that is doomed because it has been overtaken by 'progress'.

It reminded me very much of what has happened in medicine. Real, old-life doctors who cared about their patients and had a vocation for healing are treated as an anachronism. And everyone (doctors as well as patients) has lost out.

When I worked as a GP, I visited my patients at home and I visited them at night and at weekends. I worked with four other doctors and we had a rota system which meant that between us we were on call over bank holidays too – including Christmas. The days I remember most from my years in practice are the days when I managed to make a difference: to save a life by giving an injection of adrenalin, or a steroid or by getting a patient onto the appropriate ward of the appropriate hospital within 30 minutes of their calling me in the middle of the night. I had a relationship with my patients. They would stop me in the street to ask for prescriptions or tell me how they were doing. I used to get well over 100 Christmas cards (and a good many bottles of whisky) from patients every December. Doctors then were involved in proper healing. There was continuity of care and it was rewarding.

Today, GPs work on average 24 hours a week and they are deeply dissatisfied. All they get out of medicine is money. They claim to have psychological problems because they are working too hard (when they are working a fraction of the hours GPs used to work). They have walked away from their responsibilities and they have become little more than form fillers. It's no wonder that there is constant talk of strikes and walk outs and taking early retirement.

Education for children was also at its best more than 50 years ago, and for adults it reached a peak in Victorian times when educational institutes were at the centre of every town.

Travel was easier, more comfortable and more enjoyable too.

When I was a young author, travelling around the country, I could eat decent meals on trains and I could, if I wanted to, sleep on trains too. And the meals weren't dried up sandwiches and a bar of chocolate. Trains were equipped with proper dining cars, kitchens and all the appropriate staff. If I was travelling to London from the English Midlands, I could have my breakfast on the morning train and then have my dinner on the evening train coming back. The prices were very reasonable. Travel was more leisurely, more dignified and more enjoyable in the 1960s, 1970s and 1980s than it is today.

When the service began, the staff on Eurostar, from London to Paris and back again, would serve first class travellers with a full three course meal, complete with champagne, wine, coffee, chocolates and hot towels afterwards. Today, travellers are served a cafeteria style snack and are, no doubt, grateful for it. The prices have not fallen to match the standards.

Faux progress has even entered the home where property owners are being pressured to replace perfectly adequate gas fired boilers with heat pumps which cost a fortune to buy, another fortune to run and are about as useful as a candle in a thunderstorm. And sensible folk who heat their homes with log fires, have for decades been encouraged to replace perfectly decent and good looking hearths with log burners which are a modern method of making an open fire more expensive and less efficient – as well as far less pleasing – or with one of those environmentally acceptable, artificial fires with their unconvincing, flickering flames and insipid heat provided by electricity created (and here is the irony) by burning wood (that has been imported across the Atlantic on diesel burning ships) in a distant power station.

When I first started listening to music we had records which went round at 78 rpm, 45 rpm or 33 rpm. Then we were told we needed to get rid of the vinyl records and replace them with cassettes. These were conveniently small and as long as you had a pencil handy to wind back and tighten the tape occasionally, and were able to mend breaks with tiny strips of sticky tape, they were fine but not as fine as the old-fashioned records had been.

Then we were told to get rid of all our cassette tapes and replace them with CDs. This we all did, at enormous expense and inconvenience, because you couldn't buy a cassette player anymore and there weren't any new cassettes to buy.

The same thing happened with films as VHS cassette tapes were replaced by DVDs.

We were promised that CDs and DVDs were indestructible and would last forever without causing any problems whatsoever. It was all lies, of course. Moreover, it has now been proved that the sound quality with records is better than with CDs and, of course, it is much easier to read the sleeve notes on albums than it is to find anything worth looking at on the inserts included with CDs. (Why is everything printed in one point on a black background?)

CDs and DVDs seem to cause more problems than the old-fashioned cassette tapes we were encouraged to throw away. Recently, Antoinette and I have started listening to audio tapes (the full cast dramatic versions of the Lord Peter Wimsey stories by Dorothy Sayers and the Paul Temple plays by Francis Durbridge are excellent) and we've gone back to buying cassettes instead of CDs. The advantages are legion. First, of course, it is easy to stop the cassette tape exactly where you want to stop it, and to restart it the following day simply by pressing the Start button. You can't do this with CDs. Another advantage is that hardly anyone wants to buy cassette tapes and since most people only listen to audio tapes once or twice, the ones we buy are usually in excellent condition. I bought a huge pile of excellent cassettes on eBay for £25. I bought all the Sayers, all the Durbridge and most of Colin Dexter's Inspector Morse tapes. If I'd bought the CD versions they would have cost between £300 and £400. Curiously, the plastic packaging used for cassettes is slightly better than the packaging used for CDs. The jewel cases used for CDs always fall apart the minute you open them. The cases used for cassettes seem a little stronger. (The best artists insist on having their work sold in a sort of plasticised cardboard which never breaks and is much better to handle. Most artists don't care.)

I was stationary at the traffic lights when he approached. He wasn't quite a policeman (you don't see many of those walking around these days) and he was a bit more than a traffic warden. I'm not totally sure what they're called, though I'm sure they have a name; a title of some kind. They can arrest people for dropping litter or parking badly, and although I don't think they carry guns, they are laden down with the technology that all law enforcement officers carry these days: phone, camera, bullet proof vest and more leather pouches strapped to their body than a boy scout on a camping holiday.

'You don't seem to be wearing your seat belt, sir,' he said, managing to add just the right amount of official irony to the final word.

'No,' I agreed, for he was quite right. I'd been waiting for this to happen.

Antoinette wound down her window, since he was standing on the pavement on her side of the car. He looked in and gave me the two thousand yard stare they teach them before they graduate. Antoinette smiled and said 'hello' to him.

'Would you pull up just over there please, sir,' he said, indicating a space reserved for taxis.

I did as he asked.

He walked, very slowly and deliberately, to where I was parked and looked in through Antoinette's open window.

'Neither of you appears to be wearing your seat belts,' he said. Now that he had confirmed that I was a criminal he'd dropped the 'sir'.

'No,' I agreed. I started to explain that the car, being 67-years-old was built before seat belts were introduced and didn't have them fitted.

He looked carefully at the inside of the car. 'You don't have any seat belts,' he said, ignoring me.

'No,' I agreed. I was tempted to tell him that I was just on my way to report them stolen. But I resisted the temptation.

He had unhooked his phone from his chest and, after walking to the front of the car, had keyed in the registration number. 'You don't appear to have a valid road fund licence,' he said, when he came back. He looked puzzled. He squinted at his phone. 'Nor a valid MOT certificate.'

'No, I agreed. The car is exempt.'

He studied his phone.

'Exempt?'

'Exempt,' I agreed. 'No MOT, no road tax, and no seat belts required.'

'How old did you say the vehicle was?'

'Sixty seven years,' I told him. 'It was made in 1957. January 1957 to be precise.'

He studied his phone a little longer. He was a slow reader. 'Right, sir,' he said. He seemed very disappointed and still a little confused.

But I was clearly no longer a criminal. He looked down at the piece of road where we were parked. 'You'd better move on, sir,' he said sternly. 'You're parked in a space reserved for taxis.'

'Right you are, officer,' I said. I put the car into gear and we slid away gracefully.

Very few modern homes have working fireplaces and chimneys but I wouldn't buy a house which did not have an open fireplace. When the gas and electricity are turned off and there is no way to heat a property or to cook food, the people whose homes have at least one open fireplace will have an enormous advantage. They will have an even greater advantage if they also have a supply of logs which they can burn.

Log burners have been heavily promoted but they are far less efficient than open fires and I suspect they are invented and promoted by the sort of people who invented and promoted tortoiseshell condoms, alcohol free beer and decaffeinated coffee. The unanswerable question is: why bother? You get far more heat from an open fire than from a log burner and you can watch the flames too. One of the joys of lighting a real fire is the ability to watch dancing flames. The log burner shuts away the flames and denies the observer any delight at all. Log burners can be summed up succinctly as 'no view and very little heat'.

We burn our own trees. They delight us when they are alive and they warm us after they die. This is the ultimate in recycling. We have to hire tree surgeons to chop down large trees (I don't trust myself with a chain saw) but I can saw up branches and save twigs for kindling. A decent sized tree will provide us with logs and kindling for the winter. What I wonder do those who oppose open fires suggest be done with all the fallen trees? If they aren't used for burning then gardens, roads and the countryside will soon be cluttered up with dead trunks and branches.

I love all the paraphernalia associated with real fires: andirons, dogs, hearths and all the tools (pokers, tongs, brush, shovel). I love using an extendable brass toasting fork. I like to keep yule logs for Christmas and special occasions. For me the phrase 'log on' simply means building up the fire and has nothing whatsoever to do with computers.

I wouldn't buy a house without a fireplace. And if I had to choose between having a fireplace and having a TV set with a DVD player, it would be an easy decision – I'd choose the one which gives both warmth and entertainment.

Back in 1976, in my second book 'Paper Doctors', I argued that there was no need for any more medical research. I pointed out that the world's medical libraries were full of research results which had never been used. I explained that if we utilised what we knew, the quality of health care could be improved dramatically.

Naturally, the plea was ignored. Academics earn kudos and huge amounts of money by doing research, and drug companies rely on medical research to find new variations on existing drugs. (Very few new drugs of value have been discovered in the last 50 years).

And so researchers have raced ahead. There has been much work on cloning humans, on genetic engineering involving plants and animals, on the development of robots, on artificial intelligence, on techniques for euthanasia and on new ways of producing experimental vaccines. No debate or discussion is allowed on any of these developments. Anyone even daring to offer mild criticism, or suggesting that there should be debate, is dismissed with scorn as a Luddite. The search for something new, for the holy grail of progress, is unending.

Meanwhile, health care has steadily deteriorated and life expectation for both men and women is now falling. Life expectation will never again be as high as it is today.

Progress (or what we are led to believe is progress) has given us oppression, compliance, dependence and the loss of romance, humour, respect and dignity. It has replaced those things with sanctimoniousness and a sense of entitlement. Progress has helped to teach us that everything should be free but, at the same, without real value.

The more I've thought about it the more I have become convinced that cars which were built in the 1950s were better built, more reliable (and more easily repaired when they developed faults), than cars built in 2024.

And I have decided that motor cars weren't the only things that were better built. Houses built in the 1950s are still standing, still comfortable, still very habitable and infinitely better built than houses erected in the second and third decades of the 21st century.

It's true that modern public buildings have better access for the disabled than public buildings which were built years ago but I don't believe there is a public building erected in the last five decades which is as sturdy, as well designed and as well built as the public buildings erected in Queen Victoria's reign in the 19th century.

There were no mobile phones and no personal computers around in the 1950s but things were undeniably more efficient then, than they are now.

And cars built in the 1950s have more style and more class than anything built in the subsequent years.

While out driving in the Bentley, we hit a huge pothole. The car shook and I'm worried that we must have damaged something. If we have then we probably won't know for a few weeks when something will suddenly snap. By that time, of course, it will be far too late to sue the council for the damage done.

Britain spends huge amounts of money on its public services but in every area the money is largely wasted. Everyone knows that Britain's roads are crumbling, that 1,000 trains are cancelled every day because the track and the rolling stock are falling apart (and the staff are constantly on strike), and the State managed health service has collapsed and is beyond repair, but not many people realise that the country's defences are in an equally bad way.

At a time when politicians are constantly talking about a new World War (with Russia, with China and in the Middle East) Britain's armed services are little more than a joke. Britain spends £50 billion a year on its armed forces (that is 2.3% of GDP and above the average for NATO countries) but a big chunk of that is simply wasted and a fifth goes on nuclear weapons. The result is that the arms companies, and a number of former civil servants and army officers, have become exceedingly rich but the country is left with a broken catapult and a malfunctioning pea shooter with which to defend itself (or, more likely, to become an aggressor). Our navy has fewer destroyers and frigate than France, and our army has shrunk so dramatically that generals, desperate for more squaddies to shout at, are talking about conscription and some form of press ganging. During a recent NATO exercise, Britain's two aircraft carriers both broke down. One had a corroded shaft coupling and the other had a fuel leak. It was probably just as well that the ships couldn't sail because the navy's last main support ship was laid up in dock (despite a recent refit). When a Royal Navy submarine tried to test fire a Triden missile, the test was a pathetic failure. This wouldn't be so bad but it was the second test to be a failure. The missile landed close to the launch site. The admirals responsible for these fiascos should be fired but they won't be, of course. Public servants are never fired. Everyone responsible always receives a promotion, a bonus, an honour (a knighthood or a peerage) and an invitation to a garden party at Buckingham Palace (recently renovated at taxpayers' expense at a cost of around £350 million).

Politicians talk aggressively as though they were still living in the 19th century when Britain ruled the Empire and the waves but today Britain has a trio of armed services to match its failed health service.

The ageing process varies with cars, as it does with people.

Some folk are lucky and can get well into their 80s without noticing much in the way of deterioration, while others suffer terribly from a whole range of illnesses with the result that they never feel quite well, and know the receptionists at their local doctor's surgery so thoroughly that they know the names of their children, grandchildren and pets. And probably send them all birthday cards.

When I was young it was said that cars which broke down a good deal were 'Friday cars' and that they were constantly breaking down because they had been built on a Friday, when the people on the assembly line were looking forward to the weekend and not paying proper attention.

Maybe people who have a good many health problems should be referred to as 'Friday people'.

The Bentley's traffic indicators are quite modern (the usual flashing lights on all four corners, rather than the wonderful signal arms which used to come out of the sides of old cars) and they work perfectly well. Flashing lights appear on the instrument panel to tell me which indicator is switched on. However, instead of turning off automatically when the car stops turning (as happens with more modern vehicles), the indicators are controlled by a clockwork timer. After 15 seconds or so the switch is supposed to return to the off position and turn off the indicators. Sadly, the clockwork switch no longer works so I have to remember to turn off the indicator manually. Since this is a Bentley, the sound telling me that the indicator is working is extremely non-intrusive and I do sometimes forget to turn it off. It doesn't help, of course, that I'm used to indicators automatically cancelling themselves. I offer my abject apologies to all those motorists who have travelled behind me wondering why the idiot driver hasn't turned off his indicator.

A friend has a classic car which has no working indicators at all. He used to wind down his window and use the old-fashioned hand signal to indicate that he was turning right (he stuck his arm out of the window and hoped it didn't get taken off at the shoulder by a passing lorry) but found that the signal for turning left (sticking his arm out and rotating it) seemed to confuse other motorists who probably thought he was waving to a friend or being rude. He eventually got round this problem by avoiding all left hand turns. He insists that this is surprisingly easy to do.

Since we've done around £10,000 work on the car, and there is more to come, it seemed wise to increase the insurance to £30,000.

Before we bought the Bentley, I suspected that the insurance wouldn't be very expensive and for once I was correct in this apparently optimistic expectation. A call to our broker resulted in a quote for comprehensive cover for £308.99 which includes free, full RAC breakdown cover. The price is considerably less than the insurance cost for a much cheaper modern 1 litre car, and the RAC membership promised to be useful since the manufacturer's warranty ran out a few decades ago.

The broker quoted me an increase of £50 extra to take the insurance cover up to £30,000.

The insurance for the Bentley is a third of the cost of the insurance for our Maserati (which is now written down to under £30,000 in value) and half the cost of the insurance for our Mitsubishi L200 truck.

The frequently revisited attempt to ban drivers over the age of 60, 65 or 70 is based on the grounds that they have more accidents. This isn't difficult to disprove. We have three cars: a Maserati, a Mitsubishi L200 truck which we use whenever we go into town since it is, believe it or not, the narrowest of our three vehicles, and the Bentley. The total cost of comprehensive insurance for all three vehicles is under £2,000 a year whereas the average cost for an ordinary, probably smaller and cheaper family car is well over £2,000. For younger drivers the cost of third party insurance for an old banger will probably be well over £3,000 and for anything more expensive is likely to be £30,000 or even more.

Insurance companies may be crooked but they are not stupid: they charge the biggest fees to the people most likely to have accidents. If any age group needs to be banned from driving it is the under 30s.

Car owners have been told that they can reduce their car insurance, and collect brownie points for their social credit score, by having a black box fitted in their car which monitors their speed, how sharply they brake, how well they drive round corners and, of course, where they go and when they go there.

Have a black box fitted and you'll pay less for your insurance but the authorities will know exactly where you are any given moment.

How normal is it to feel tired at 70, at 80, at 90?

I have absolutely no idea what is normal and what is not normal because I've never been here before.

I have difficulty opening jars. The child safety feature means I cannot open most jars and bottles. I drew attention to this problem in articles when I was a young GP and now I'm caught by it. I have to use a cloth or a gripper to get the damned things undone.

I get tired easily. If I walk to our bonfire site with a bag of garden rubbish I have to stop and rest two or three times.

And I was always much stronger. I have difficulty in picking up a bag of logs for the fire.

Is it all a sign of some developing disorder?

Or is it just my age?

I dunno.

I've never been 77 before.

There was a time when the travelling was as important as the arriving.

Victorian travellers who had to cover the miles by (horse drawn) coach or by train, and who could take days, weeks or even months to reach their destination, did not regard the travelling as a waste of time. They regarded the travelling as being a significant part of their experience. I doubt if many people still think that way. The older you are, and the longer you have been travelling, the more likely you are to find modern travel unpleasant and something to be avoided whenever possible.

Today, everyone who travels is treated like a criminal. Photographs and finger prints are taken and stored. If the majority of people stood up and said No to this nonsense it wouldn't happen. But most people don't say a word in protest and so it happens. It is part of the new 'social credit' programme.

Putting aside the queues, the security nightmares, the uncertainties, the delays, the terrible food, the lost baggage, the inevitable strikes, the crowded aeroplanes and the fact that you are quite likely to have your belongings confiscated for no good reason whatsoever, the fundamental problem with travelling by air is that there is no real sense of travelling at all. The traveller goes to an airport and then a few hours or a few days later, arrives at another almost identical airport in a different country. And, whatever the destination, the chances are that apart from the temperature and the weather there will be little difference in the hotels and the food. These days no one enjoys the journey – wherever they are going. And modern travel, usually by aeroplane, takes us to our destination without our minds or bodies having the chance to acclimatise.

Travel is no longer an adventure, an essential part of the overall experience; it is now merely a burden, the price to be paid for the prize of reaching your destination. We have been taught to believe that it is only the destination that matters, although traditionally the journey was always important. The Victorians used to do Grand Tours of Europe that consisted of very little but travelling.

We had an apartment in central Paris for twenty years and in the end, with some sadness, we sold it, partly because the difficulty of getting there (and back) took away the joy of being there. Air travel became impossible because of the vast amount of time that had to be wasted going through customs. The waiting was interminable. And then railway travel, via Eurostar, became unbearable for much the same reason.

Over a century ago, writers such a Thackeray used to travel to Paris quite regularly. So did Arnold Bennett and H.G.Wells. Today, foreign travel is infinitely more expensive, more tiresome, more exhausting than it used to be. It probably takes longer to get to Paris now than it took a century ago.

Having given up going abroad, I would very much like to travel more in Britain. There is a great deal I still wish to see, and it astonishes me that so many people who insist on taking all their holidays abroad know so very little of their own island. (The same thing goes, of course, for those who live in the US, France or Italy.) I'd love to visit all the Scottish castles, climb all the Munros (or struggle up them) and visit all the remaining English piers. I probably won't, however, because the trains in Britain are unreliable and the train drivers seem to be forever calling strikes, the roads are packed with speed cameras, confusing road signs, pot holes and traffic jams. And, because hardly anyone uses trains any more, far too much traffic. It has been proved, by the way, that speed cameras cause accidents. They are clearly put in position simply to raise money for the authorities.

On top of that, hotels in Britain are appalling. Most are unwelcoming and cold in every sense, have too few members of staff, change towels and sheets only when they have to and produce food that is barely edible and served in mean portions. I ordered a cooked breakfast in one five star hotel and received a solitary half a grilled tomato, naked under a metal cover. At another posh hotel, my lemon tea arrived with no lemon. When I murmured gently about the omission, the waiter removed the teapot lid and showed me a whole lemon floating inside. At another expensive, five star hotel, the chef refused to cook potatoes at all because he felt they were beneath him. He clearly also had no idea how to feed vegetarians and so we were given a few greens and nothing else. The manager proudly told us that the chef (who clearly regarded himself as being far more important than the guests) also refused to have teacakes in the hotel, so our afternoon tea was miserable until we realised we could go out to a bakery, buy teacakes and butter and eat them cold in our room.

The absurd employment laws in Britain mean that local hotels are much more expensive than anywhere else in the world and this probably helps explain why so many people put up with the pain of travelling abroad in order to take their holidays outside Britain. We've tried renting cottages but generally speaking that has been unsuccessful too. Most are badly furnished and the owners are clearly only interested in obeying the rules and regulations set by bodies which hand out rosettes and stars.

We did rather fancy travelling about in a motor caravan so that we could look after ourselves but then we would still have to deal with the pot holed roads jam packed with traffic. We did buy a caravan but we haven't yet managed to use it. It is, however, an excellent repository for all the accounts which the tax people insist that I keep. Since I'm self-employed, I am advised that I need to keep all my records for twenty years. So I do. We used to keep the paperwork in the garage but the damp and the mice made that a poor storage place. The price of a good caravan is much lower than the price of a purpose built shed – and easier to keep warm and dry if necessary. You can also sleep, wash and cook in it if your home catches fire. And one of these fine days we'll hitch it up to the tow-bar on the back of our truck and tow it off to some distant spot on a patch of sheep-mown grass beside a babbling brook.

These days we rarely travel further than we can safely manage to reach in an hour or so, meaning that we can get back home without having to stay the night somewhere.

And an elderly Bentley suits our needs very well.

Before we gave up travelling, I used to think it would be good to revisit places we've enjoyed in the past. But that rarely works. The place we remember with such affection will have changed dramatically since we were there last. And, more importantly, what we remember with such joy is not the physical place but the mood, the experience, the circumstances and so on. And you can't recreate those simply by going back to the same spot.

I noticed today that there is a little rust appearing on the chromium plated air grills just above the Bentley's front bumper. I have ordered some magic stuff that if painted onto the rust will remove it and restore the chrome to its original state. I have no doubt that it is probably also being sold as a cure for eczema, a reliable way of killing aphids and a potion to get rid of wrinkles. There will apparently be a slight delay before the stuff arrives because it is coming from China. I have already purchased a small bottle of touch up paint (in the correct Bentley colour) so that when the weather is a little more reliable I can deal with any chip marks. And I have bought some leather in the correct colour so that I can put a patch across the cuts in the front seat.

I have never tinkered with a car before and I have still not given up the idea that one day I will be able to do something under the bonnet. I am, however, already further forward in that direction than I have ever been before in that I can, with comparative ease, now operate the levers which operate the two halves of the bonnet.

Meanwhile, I have already done a couple of useful things which have given me some confidence.

When the car arrived, the petrol filler flap would not open and the boot was stuck shut. I succeeded in opening the petrol cap by (very gently) tapping it and then encouraging it to open with the blade of a penknife. (Please don't tell anyone I did this. If you do then I am afraid I shall deny it and insist that you misinterpreted what I had written.) And I succeeded in opening the boot by pulling very, very hard on the handle.

I had (correctly) guessed that the petrol filler flap was stuck simply because it hadn't been used for a long time. And I had (also correctly) guessed that the boot was stuck because the rubber seal had perished slightly.

Both guesses were absolutely accurate. The petrol filler flap now opens perfectly, as does the boot. I have removed all the rubber seal and in due course I'll glue it back into place.

I'm really quite proud of my skills as a car mechanic Class 3.

I have earned my living as a professional author for most of my life and authors all agree that the first question strangers ask is usually 'What name do you write under?'

The question makes it clear that they've never heard of you and that you cannot, therefore, be very successful.

John Baxter (who has written beautiful books about Paris and about book collecting) says that an author he knows always responds with 'Name some writers and I'll tell you if I'm one of them.'

The questioner cannot usually think of the names of any authors except Shakespeare, Dickens and maybe someone who is on the telly a lot and puts his or her name to ghost written gardening or cookery books for the Christmas market.

The other question people ask authors is: 'Can you make a living at it?'

This is also patronising and dismissive.

The thing is, of course, that everyone thinks that they could write books if they only had the time.

Playwright Arthur Miller (author of Death of a Salesman and one time husband of Marilyn Monroe) tells how he once bought a hotdog in the street and noticed that the vendor was someone with whom he was at school.

'So, what are you doing now, Artie?' asked the man.

'I write plays,' said Miller.

'Playwriting,' said the hotdog seller thoughtfully. 'Yeah. I should have gone into that.'

The thing about writing books for a living is that you really need to be persistent (unless you know someone in the business). Just about every famous, successful author collected dozens if not hundreds of rejection slips before they succeeded in finding an agent or publisher prepared to handle their first book. John Creasey, the world's most prolific writer of detective stories, had 743 rejection slips before he managed to sell his first book. But once the gates were open his output was phenomenal. He published 564 novels under 25 pseudonyms. On average each book took him 26 days. Novelist Fay Weldon admitted that for 20 years everything she wrote was rejected. It took HG Wells six years to get published. Agatha Christie, Anita Loos, Alan Sillitoe, Irwin Shaw, Tennessee Williams, Beatrix Potter, James Joyce, Sinclair Lewis and hundreds of other famous authors had famous and subsequently successful books rejected. J.P.Donleavy's bestseller 'The Ginger Man' was rejected 45 times. Lorna Doone by RD Blackmore was turned down 18 times. Peyton Place by Grace Metalious was rejected 14 times and 'How to win friends and influence people' by Dale Carnegie was sent back 17 times.

I sometimes wonder how publishers ever manage to make any money. The publisher who turned down Catch 22 by Joseph Heller complained 'I haven't really the foggiest idea about what this man is trying to say' and the publisher who turned down 'The spy who came in from the cold' by John Le Carre said: 'You're welcome to le Carre – he hasn't got any future'.

On more than one occasion, frustrated authors have typed out famous and incredibly successful books and then submitted them to see what publishers would say. The books, whether classics or modern bestsellers, are invariably rejected.

These days, life for budding authors is somewhat easier. No one needs a publisher and a year-long wait to put a book into production. Websites such as Amazon allow authors to publish their own books, design their own covers and put their books up for sale almost immediately.

I can understand why so many young people don't bother to learn to drive. The roads are becoming increasingly impossible. The rapid growth in immigration means that all roads (even once quiet country lanes) are massively overcrowded while motorways are more like car parks than thoroughfares.

Cyclists and pedestrians now have priority on British roads with the result that motorists who do not allow five feet of space when overtaking cyclists can be prosecuted (on country lanes this means that motorists who overtake must put their offside wheels on the grass verge in order to do so without fear of prosecution). Road furniture, designed to block and slow traffic and to create traffic jams is a constant annoyance, as are the extra payments which must be paid when a motorist dares to drive into a town or city. The prospect of driverless cars is even more alarming since on Britain's narrow roads, with blind corners every few miles, the chances are that the driverless vehicles will remain rooted to the spot indefinitely, with queues behind them stretching for miles. It is difficult to avoid the thought that what is happening is deliberate, and all part of the plan that we must all stop travelling and stick in one spot in our 15 or 20 minute city.

The S1 is a perfect example of the point when cars reached their limit: the point when they became as complicated as they needed to be. Cars which were made later are far too complicated for their own good and certainly far too complex for their drivers.

The S1 was fitted with an automatic gearbox and power steering. The windscreen wipers can be set to go slow or fast and there is a windscreen washer too. (The owner's handbook says, rather proudly I think: 'A vacuum operated device enables the driver to wash the windscreen whilst driving the car'.) There is air conditioning and a heater (both of which are easily operated with neat and easy to operate Bentley buttons and both of which work extraordinarily well) and a rear window demister (with the on/off switch curiously situated on the parcel shelf behind the back seat).

The steering feels incredibly loose when compared to modern cars but this was done deliberately so that if the chauffeur or owner driver (and this was one of the first Bentley motor cars to be designed with the thought the owner might drive it himself) suddenly sneezed, the car would not suddenly be wafted from the straight and narrow. The slight disadvantage, of course, is that the driver has to whirl the steering wheel round and round, if he needs to go round a hairpin bend or manoeuvre into a parking space.

I really believe that the Bentley S marked the apogee for motor car production.

Modern cars are fitted with too many gadgets. We have a

Maserati which, like many modern cars, switches on its own headlamps when darkness falls and switches on the windscreen wipers if a raindrop hits the windscreen. If one of the tyres loses a little air, a warning sign lets us know which tyre needs attention. There is so much electric stuff in the car that the battery has to be recharged once a fortnight. And things go wrong without any obvious explanation. This morning I went downstairs to find that overnight the car had decided to open all four windows. We were lucky that it hadn't been raining. We were luckier that the squirrels hadn't decided to turn the car's interior into a super-dray.

Overcomplicated cars make life harder not easier. We had a car (a very powerful four wheel drive Jeep Cherokee) which was fitted with a vast array of complex electronics but when we hit a large pothole on the M6, everything disappeared and we didn't even know how fast we were travelling. Much the same thing happened with a quite new BMW 7 series which we had. None of the engineers who looked at the car could solve the problem which we ended up having to give away as scrap.

Our Bentley still has wind up (and down) windows, and this was one of the reasons why we chose the S type rather than the S2 which had electric windows fitted.

Electric windows are something else to go wrong and are incredibly difficult to repair. They are almost impossible to replace in an old car and even in new cars they can be a constant source of problems and irritations. The Jeep Cherokee which we had, developed an incredibly inconvenient problem when the electric windows wouldn't go up and down. Moreover, while two doors wouldn't open, the other two wouldn't lock. It turned out that rain had got into the motors inside the doors and had damaged them. The window winding motors had actually gone rusty because, as the manager of the garage pointed out: 'I had driven the car in the rain'. It had never occurred to me that a sturdy looking four wheel drive car would be allergic to rain and unsuitable for use in wet weather. The cost of replacing the motors was, of course, considerable. Buying the Jeep was a sign that I have difficulty in learning since it was the second Jeep Cherokee I've owned and the first was also a disaster. I bought it brand new and it was already rusty.

I've had several modern cars where very simple faults were impossible to deal with without a day's work. Just replacing a headlight bulb, for example, can take a day in a specialist garage. And this isn't just something that happens to me. I recently read about a problem that developed when a Ford F-150 pick-up truck had a failed rear light. This is a common problem with motor vehicles but repairing the light cost $5,600. The electronic complexity of modern vehicles means that the light is connected to many other parts of the truck, and diagnosing and treating the problem is far more complicated than it should be. The end result of this is that many perfectly serviceable motor cars are thrown away because the cost of a quite small and simple repair is so great that the car isn't worth repairing. This is a particularly common problem when cars are involved in relatively minor accidents. Is this because the car industry doesn't care about the long-term problems buyers are likely to face? Or is it simply part of the programme of planned obsolescence which has been part of life for the last half a century or more?

It has been suggested that we need more innovative and imaginative engineers who are able to repair broken down cars and put them back on the road (as happened in Cuba in the 1950s when the streets were awash with American cars which had been junked and which had found a new life) but the problem is that rules and regulations mean that this is unlikely to happen these days.

The fact is that the handles which allow us to lower and raise the windows in the Bentley S type are simple, fast and easy to operate. They're a little stiff through disuse but they'll soon loosen up. We even have old-fashioned quarter lights and although I recognise that back in the 1950s and 1960s these were regarded by car thieves as quite useful points of access, I rather doubt if modern car thieves would have any idea how to open one.

Our Maserati, like many other modern cars can do scores of things I don't want it to do or need it to do. The car will tell me exactly when it needs a new service, and if I don't go to an authorised dealer the notification will remain there forever; an eternally irritating reminder that I have probably destroyed the value of my warranty.

The other advantage of having less stuff powered by electricity is that the battery doesn't keep running down. Modern cars, especially expensive ones, have so much electrically operated equipment that their batteries are constantly running down. So, as a result, a modern

Bentley must have its battery plugged into a mains socket once a fortnight or so in order to keep it alive. If we don't plug in our Maserati every fortnight there is a real danger that the battery will die. And since the battery can only be reached via the boot and the boot can only be opened electronically, I have no idea what we will do if the battery goes flat. Many modern cars are also equipped with a ridiculously stupid Stop/Start feature which automatically cuts out the engine if the vehicle stops for more than a moment or two. The engine is automatically started again when it's time to proceed. The strain on the battery and the starter motor must be colossal if a car is stuck in a long traffic jam. The idea, I assume, is to save a teaspoonful of petrol every time the engine is turned off. The worst thing about this gimmick is that it seems to be a default setting. There is one of these daft buttons on our Maserati and I have to turn it off every time I start the car.

All this complicated stuff is often beyond the skill of garage mechanics too. Back in the 1990s I had a Volvo estate car which had a two speed wiper on the back window and little wipers fitted to the headlamps. After a front end shunt (a pony leapt out of the dark while I was driving across Exmoor and landed on the bonnet before scrambling off and galloping away) I took the car into a small local garage to be repaired. The owner of the garage was a lovely bloke but not terribly adept with new technology. I once found him wandering around the streets near to his garage looking for a particular model of Audi and hoping that the owner would let him take a look at the engine to see where something was supposed to be fitted. When I collected the Volvo after it had been repaired, the owner of the garage told me that he hadn't been able to stop the headlamp wipers from operating constantly. 'But don't worry,' he said with a grin, 'I managed to solve it. I cut the wires and that stopped them.'

All these complications result in people constantly needing expert help. The more things there are to go wrong, the more things will go wrong. And the modern motorist is encouraged to believe that everything must work at all times. Indeed, if he doesn't make sure that everything is working as it ought to work there is a danger that his insurance company will consider the insurance policy invalid. And the black box which his shiny new car probably carries will doubtless report everything to the insurance company. Even cars snitch on their owners these days.

There are many disadvantages in being old. But there are some advantages.

They can't send you to prison for 40 years, and a life sentence doesn't have quite the sting at 77 as it would have at 25.

No one expects you to be able to lift or carry heavy things or, indeed, do anything strenuous.

No one complains if you suddenly fall asleep.

No one is too startled if you forget where you are, where you've been or where you are supposed to be.

You can blame borborygmi, etc., on the dog and people will pretend to believe you, even if you haven't got a dog.

Right from the start we have had a little trouble with the door locks which need a little attention. I have tried a number of locksmiths but none of them can help. The car specialists all say they don't deal with locks and the locksmiths all say they don't deal with cars.

And I'm also having difficulty having a spare ignition key made. When we had a new (reconditioned) ignition box it came with just one key. Locksmiths couldn't find a suitable blank. Eventually, I managed to buy the correct blank for £30 from a specialist supplier. I took the key that works and the blank to a branch of Timpson's and asked the guy behind the counter to copy the key.

But he said he couldn't.

'We can't cut a key with a blank we don't supply. We don't know what the metal is.'

I pointed out that the blank was an official, proper Bentley blank.

He wouldn't budge.

There are rules everywhere these days.

I would rather have our minor problem with the old Bentley's locks than the problem we had with the modern, streamlined, aerodynamic and definitely rather whizzy looking Bentley Continental we had a few years back.

The car was, as you might expect, fitted with all the folderols that teams of engineers could think of (and probably some that were lifted straight from one of those Marvel magazines about super heroes) and I regret to say that during our ownership, I never got close to finding out what could, or could not, be done. There was a manual and instructions were available and I'm sure that my problems were all my fault. I just didn't have a spare six months to study the instructions.

But it was the door locks which defeated me. The car was fitted with some sort of primitive brain which enabled it to tell when someone holding the key (or with the key in a pocket or bag) was nearby. I never really knew whether or not the car was supposed to do this but the locks would spring open upon my approach. This was very impressive but there was a problem. When I left the car in a car park, and had locked the car with the key, I would walk away. As anyone would. But since I was still holding the key when I had locked the car the locks would then click open again, ready for me to climb in and drive away even though I didn't want to get in and drive away.

To begin with, I tried locking the car and then running off as fast as I could, in the hope that the car would not register that I was still there. But that didn't work because I couldn't run fast enough to outwit the car. I'd lock the car and scurry off and the mechanical brain would recognise my presence, think I wanted to get into the car, and unlock the doors. Eventually I learned that if I locked the car from a distance I could get away fast enough to stop the car opening the doors again. I then had to put the keys on the ground and go back to the car to check that the doors were still locked.

I have no doubt that this performance provided other motorists with some entertainment but eventually I tired of it, and we sold the car.

I'm ready to admit, by the way, that this was undoubtedly all my fault. I probably hadn't pressed the correct buttons in the correct sequence. Although there must be a chance that there was some sort of (whisper it quietly) fault.

But I much prefer the old-fashioned key that comes with the Bentley S1. The driver's door doesn't open until I put the key in the lock and wiggle it about. And then I have to go round and open the front passenger door with the key. When we leave the car, I simply wiggle the key in the lock and try the handle to see if the door is locked.

Daft speed limits and speed restriction nonsenses mean that it now takes longer to travel in London than in 387 other cities in 55 countries. London is now the slowest city in the world for the second year in succession – after the introduction of the absurd 20 mph speed limits. It takes on average 37 minutes and 20 seconds to travel 6.2 miles in London. That is the average. It can take an hour or more to travel a mile. It is, perhaps, no wonder that productivity is lower in Britain than almost anywhere else in the world.

I used to enjoy trips to London, and when I edited a medical journal, I stayed there once a week in a room at the National Liberal Club in Whitehall. Then for decades I travelled there regularly to meet editors and make television or radio programmes, though that all seems a lifetime ago.

However, Antoinette and I haven't been to London for years. Moving about takes forever, the city is filthy dirty and incredibly noisy, hardly anyone speaks English (so experiences in cafes and shops are tiring), taxi drivers are always glum and depressing and constant train strikes mean that every visit is likely to end up with hours spent waiting at one of London's gloomy mainline stations. I used to drive to London and park in a huge car park underneath Hyde Park. But I have no idea what permits are necessary in order to drive into the city.

I used to miss London very much. Today, I don't miss it at all and I may never go there again.

We parked the Bentley in a surprisingly quiet car park (it was February in a seaside resort town) and I went off to feed all my change into the nearest machine. When I got back Antoinette had opened the boot to take out a bag.

'Look!' she whispered, pointing.

I looked but couldn't see anything other than the inside of a boot. The main part of the boot contained the car cover we've never used.

The lower part of the boot contained the spare wheel and the jack, which was wrapped in an old towel so that it didn't make a noise if it moved around. There's no point in having the quietest car in the world if the jack is forever bouncing around in the boot.

'There's a mouse in there!' said Antoinette, pointing to the part of the boot where the spare wheel and jack are stored.

I looked more closely and could see that the towel around the jack had been chewed and there were leaves mixed in with what was left of the cloth. Since I knew I hadn't filled the boot with leaves, and I didn't think it likely that Antoinette had either, it was a fair guess that there was something living in the boot and that the something had made a nest there.

I reached out and moved the jack slightly.

And a mouse jumped out and raced across the deserted car park at a speed that would have won it the gold medal at the Mouse Olympics. If it had been of human being size it would have been travelling at around 150 mph.

But, sadly for the mouse, it wasn't fast enough.

A crow appeared out of nowhere, swooped, and before we could call out a warning, the mouse was lunch.

I wonder still how on earth the mouse got into the boot. Did it pick the lock? Is there some secret passageway? And how many other mice are living in there? (When you find one mouse somewhere it won't be a lone mouse. Coleman's first and only law of mice is that there's always more than one.)

We were both incredibly sad about it. The crow got a good meal but it would have been happy with a few discarded chips or half an ice cream. The mouse had found itself a warm spot for the winter and now it didn't ever have to worry again about being cold.

For some reason which I cannot explain I was reminded of a story I heard Spike Milligan tell on a television talk show.

Milligan was a great friend of Peter Sellers (they were both members of the team which brought us the Goons) and by the time of the story, Sellers had become rich and famous and had bought himself a Rolls Royce.

As they drove through central London, Sellers suddenly felt that he could hear a rattle coming from somewhere at the rear of the car. 'You drive,' he said to Milligan, 'I'll get in the boot and see if I can work out where the noise is coming from and what it is.'

So, Sellers climbed into the boot, Milligan shut the boot lid, got behind the wheel and drove off.

Five minutes later he was stopped by a policeman, who obviously didn't think Milligan looked like a Rolls Royce owner or even a chauffeur.

'Is this your car, sir?' asked the copper. (They were polite in those days.)

'No, it belongs to Peter Sellers,' said Milligan.

'And where is Mr Sellers?' asked the policeman.

'He's in the boot,' replied Milligan.

You can imagine the rest.

Sellers insisted that he had been car-jacked and thrown into the boot. The policeman called for help and arrested Milligan and it took hours to sort it all out.

I still feel sad about the mouse. But, although he was fast he was just not fast enough.

Today I put some petrol into the Bentley and worked out that we have been getting around 14 mpg. This is much higher than I expected, particularly since all our journeys have been short ones. When new, the Bentley S type was expected to get around the same. This rather suggests to me that the engine is in pretty good condition.

'All I want to know is where I am going to die, so I'll never go there.'
Charlie Munger

The older I get the more I realise that the words 'logical' and 'inevitable' are fiendishly overrated. Consider this: when a 'sparkling perry' drink called Babycham was first introduced in the 1950s, it was promoted as a champagne substitute and suitable for young men to buy for sophisticated, young women. Sadly, for the makers, Babycham sold rather poorly.

And then someone decided to quadruple the price. Usually when a product doesn't sell the sensible thing to do is to reduce the price. But the people in charge put up the price.

After the dramatic price increase, the sales then took off.

Who'd have thought it?

I reckon the reason was that young men didn't want to be seen buying a cheap product for their girlfriends but that when the price went up they were happy to buy it.

And here's another oddity: looking through old medical books I see that cigarette consumption rose after the connection with lung cancer was first suggested.

Why was that?

Bravado?

Or was the advertising from the cigarette companies more convincing than the warnings in the media? Who knows.

In 1814, a huge 50 stone iron hoop slipped. This was important because the hoop was helping to hold together a giant barrel filled with 100,000 gallons of beer. The hoop fell off and the barrel burst. The bursting barrel knocked the bung out of its neighbouring barrel. And within minutes, a 15 foot high flood of beer was sweeping through a London slum. The disaster, now forgotten, killed more people than the Great Fire of London.

We receive a constant stream of begging letters from charities but Antoinette and I don't give much to the big charities these days.

Too many big charities spend most of their money on absurdly exaggerated salaries (and the absurdly exaggerated pensions that go with them) and on massive expense accounts for their executives. Many big charities spend three quarters of their income on staff overheads and on maintaining unnecessarily smart offices. Take out marketing costs, and there is next to nothing left to spend on the alleged purpose of the charity. Plus, I don't understand why so many charities feel they need to have posh offices in an expensive part of central London.

We used to give tons of stuff to charities (and we still give books and DVDs, etc., to local ones which support hospices and so on) but we have little faith in large national charities which pay obscenely huge salaries to executives, spend a fortune on expensive offices, pay no local taxes, employ few or no local people and charge more for second-hand goods than some shops charge for new goods. Bizarrely, it is cheaper to buy second-hand books off eBay than from charity shops – even though many of the books sold online are sold by charities.

Instead, with a few exceptions, we generally prefer to give to individuals who are deserving, or who need a little help. And in cafes and at Christmas we always tip over generously.

In his wonderful novel 'Henry Ryecroft', George Gissing describes how his hero meets a small boy sobbing his heart out. The boy is distraught because he lost sixpence with which he was entrusted to perform an errand. Ryecroft reaches into his own pocket and gives the boy sixpence to replace the lost coin. He described the moment as 'his sixpenny miracle' and rejoices that he could afford to ease the boy's pain. 'I have known the day,' he writes, 'when it would have been beyond my power altogether, or else would have cost me a meal. Wherefore let me again be glad and thankful.'

In Ireland many, many generations ago, 'seanchais' were employed to recall and share the lessons of the past. Poets and story-tellers reminded the citizens of Ireland, and their leaders, of the triumphs and disasters of the great heroes of the past. The elderly were revered as a source of wisdom. Sadly this ancient tradition is now just that: a tradition. And probably a tradition soon to be forgotten.

Somewhere along the way, humans lost their sense of dignity. I suspect it's around somewhere, tucked away in a cupboard alongside respect and honour.

What a pity it is that so many public figures seem so determined to remain in the public eye that they forget about their dignity and parade themselves in public when they should be avoiding the cameras. Fading celebrities, desperate to hang onto the fame they once had, demean themselves on quiz shows and reality TV shows. (TV companies love cheap reality shows because there is no need for actors or script writers. Most of these programmes are based on the idea of the survival of the individual. Each competitor must destroy everyone else by cheating, lying and deceiving. What a great example this sets.)

And what an even bigger pity that so many relatives, friends and hangers on insist on parading famous folk in front of the cameras when they are clearly demented and to be blunt 'past their prime'. I find it difficult to avoid the painful thought that this is done to provide a little publicity, and maybe a career boost, for the relative, friend or hanger on.

I have asked Antoinette to ensure that if I ever lose or even mislay my marbles, she will refuse to allow me to publish anything or in any other way make a complete fool of myself in public.

The Duke of Wellington was so popular after his victory at Waterloo that he became Prime Minister. It probably wasn't a job for which he was well prepared. After his first Cabinet Meeting, in 1834, he said: 'An extraordinary affair. I gave them their orders and they wanted to stay and discuss them.' I don't really know why, but I love that story.

Every doctor I knew well and counted as a friend is dead.

It's 30 years since a pal of mine died at the awfully early age of 46. He was a GP. He weighed 18 stone and was five foot nine inches tall. He ate everything that was bad for him. And, as you can guess by his weight, he ate a lot of everything. Pies and chips were his daily diet. He smoked constantly and drank a bottle of wine or port every day (with half a bottle of spirits a day as a chaser). He was a happy fellow who had no real worries. I still don't understand why he behaved as he did. Did he think the rules didn't apply to him?

I knew a consultant radiologist who smoked constantly in the little room where he looked at scans and X-rays. You couldn't see across the room for the smoke. He took no notice of the rules forbidding smoking. He too died in his 40s. All such unnecessary deaths puzzle and distress me.

A dear friend who lived and worked in Australia, developed a brain cancer and lost the power of speech. I spoke to him on the telephone for a quarter of an hour a few days before he died. He couldn't answer me, of course. Have you ever tried to manage a 15 minute one way telephone conversation with someone whom you love and who is dying?

And a good chum of mine (with whom I worked when I was a GP) was misdiagnosed by one of his partners who missed a bowel cancer – even though my chum had insisted that he had a problem. When my chum eventually received treatment, the consultant screwed up with the radiotherapy and fried his bladder and ureters, with the result that he needed a catheter as well as a colostomy bag. We used to meet to drink champagne and watch cricket matches at Taunton.

‘The time indicated on the timetable is not the time at which the train will leave; it is the time before which the train will definitely not leave.'
Sign at Agra Station, India

Progress never sleeps. I see that it is now possible to buy a specially designed duster which has a long bendy handle and is advertised as being suitable for cleaning away dust which has gathered behind radiators. Surely, anyone who worries about dusting behind their radiators has far too much free time on their hands. Moreover, this is clearly discriminatory against dust. Where is dust supposed to collect if it cannot collect behind radiators without being disturbed?

There is no doubt that bureaucracy is killing Britain faster than it is killing other countries. I don't know why this is so; but it is.

And the bureaucrats who control the planning system are the most toxic and potent. We thought again about having a garage built for the Bentley, but abandoned the idea when we looked at the paperwork we'd have to deal with. We even gave up the idea of having electric gates fitted because of the rules and regulations which exist.

Britain has a byzantine planning system for major infrastructure as well as for local building works. Even the Government has to endure long waits for planning officials to reach a conclusion. For example, it now takes 4.2 years for the Government to get permission for a National Significant Infrastructure Project. That is nearly twice what it was just a few years ago. Still, the system keeps lawyers busy and rich. It is perhaps no coincidence that Britain spends less on infrastructure spending than any other G7 country. The country is literally falling apart.

And then there are all the strange pressure groups which are determined to stop good things happening. So, for example, bats are responsible for many building delays in Britain.

For reasons best known to some unknown bureaucrat, bats are more protected in Britain than anywhere else in the world. Building projects have to be halted or abandoned if bats are seen nearby. And yet there are gazillions of bats around. I love animals but protecting bats is as daft as protecting rats.

Opposition from various groups means that Britain hasn't built a new nuclear power station for 29 years and is soon going to run out of energy. Building a laboratory in Britain costs twice as much as in, say, Holland.

The problem is always the same: the number of rules and regulations which govern planning applications.

So, for example, consider the Dartford Crossing under the River Thames, which is one of the most congested roads in Europe.

For 15 years there have been plans for a new tunnel to replace the old one. The proposal is supported by locals who are fed up with long delays and the polluted air which is an inevitable consequence of permanent traffic jams. The project was designated a national priority back in 2011 but still nothing has happened except that the planning application has provided ample work for a large number of lawyers. The current planning application is 359,866 pages long and consists of 94,534,273 words. (Or at least it was when I wrote this paragraph. By now it is doubtless longer). If you tried to read it and sat still for 24 hours a day, without taking a break, it would take you a year. Just printing out the application costs £45,000 in ink. For one copy. The National Highways has spent £267 million preparing the application, though in some countries that would be enough money to pay for building the entire tunnel.

And even if the application is ever passed, and the estimated £9 billion is found to build the new tunnel, it will take 17 years to build it (though other countries would complete a similar project in three years at most and China would probably get it finished in a weekend.)

I believe books will never disappear. It is impossible for it to happen. Of all of mankind's diverse tools, undoubtedly the most astonishing are his books. All the others are extensions of the body. The telephone is an extension of his voice; the telescope and microscope extension of his sight; the word and the plough are extensions of his arms....Mankind owes all that we are to the written word... Books are the great memory of the centuries. Consequently their function is irreplaceable. If books were to disappear, history would disappear. So would men.' – Jorge Luis Borges

We have noticed that some people look when they see an elderly car passing by. And some people show no interest whatsoever.

Almost without exception the people who look are the same age as the car or older. They see an old Bentley and they remember when they saw one before. (It was probably a long time ago.) They look, I'm delighted to say, at the car not the contents and they are invariably respectful.

People under 40 almost never take any interest, even though they have probably never seen a 1957 Bentley before.

And children, who have almost certainly never seen such a car before, show absolutely no interest – though this may be because their eyes are fixed firmly to their smart phone screens and they see nothing that doesn't come to them via Apple, Samsung or some other electronic conveyance.

The Bentley is immune to the road tax but in order to waste time we still have to apply for immunity each year (as though the car were going to get younger as the years pass by).

Our Maserati and Mitsubishi truck are, sadly, not immune.

Today I received a letter from DVLA asking for £570 road tax for the Maserati. I was about to find the address so that I could send a cheque when I noticed that there were only two payment options: either online or by telephone (which will, I assume, be an automated system). In small type, however, I noticed a section headed 'Other ways to apply'. And here I found a message giving me a website to visit if I was unable 'to transact online' and wanted to send a cheque in the post. It all sounds stupid and discriminatory and ageist. But while it may be discriminatory and ageist it isn't stupid, of course. It's all part of the plan to get rid of cash, cheques and traditional bank accounts.

Robb Wilton, a legendary British radio comedian, film star and music hall artist attended a funeral and in the cemetery found himself standing next to a fellow vaudevillian Charlie Edwards. 'How old are you then, Charlie?' asked Robb. 'Ninety four,' replied Charlie. Wilton looked at him for a moment and said: 'Hardly worth your while going home, is it?'

I have come to the conclusion that there are two sets of people in this world.

There are those who believe that Sir Edmund Hilary and Sherpa Tensing were the first men to climb Everest and there are those who believe that George Mallory and Sandy Irving got there in 1924, though they died on the way down the mountain. (It was, by the way George Mallory who told an enquirer that he intended to climb Everest 'because it was there'. The remark was, I suspect, uttered in exhaustion by a man who had been asked the same damned question a million times, and was too tired to explain, again, what drove him and had run out of slick answers.)

The first group are the pragmatists who do not believe anything unless it has been officially authorised, approved and rubber stamped.

The second group are the romantics.

The first group believe that only cars which have been built according to modern government standards should be allowed on the road and that cars which were not built according to the demands from the bureaucrats should be banished.

The second group believe that classic cars add romance, delight and beauty to our roads.

Incidentally, George Mallory climbed Everest with style. He took champagne and quails eggs with him and climbed Everest in a gabardine jacket and trousers and a pair of hobnail boots.

Here's an amazing thing: Ferenc Szisz, the Hungarian born driver who won the world's first Grand Prix motor race had never before competed in a Grand Prix.

'May I look back on life as a long task duly completed – a piece of biography; faulty enough, but good as I could make it – and, with no thought but one of contentment, welcome the repose to follow when I have breathed the word 'Finis'.' – George Gissing

I don't have much interest or faith in artificial intelligence. I'll be impressed when the robot manufacturers can produce something that can play table tennis and chess. I was, however, amused when I read that a male humanoid robot had been unveiled in Saudi Arabia and had almost immediately inappropriately touched a female reporter on the bottom. Maybe there is hope for robots after all – if they can stay out of prison.

We live in a world where the rules, demands, instructions, orders and threats come by the hundred every day. 'Do not go this way'. 'Do not park here'. 'Wear a mask'. Get vaccinated'. 'Fill in this form.' 'Buy a licence for this.' 'Buy a licence for that.'

Even visits to shops are stressful because there are signs everywhere warning customers that if they are disrespectful to staff then they will be punished or banned or reported to some higher authority. Moreover, they will be punished if they say something which is, or might be, considered disrespectful to women, homosexuals, transsexuals or people of another colour or race. And they will be reported to the police if they use derogatory language (whatever that is) or wolf whistle (heaven forbid).

There are, however, no rules forbidding staff members from being rude to customers.

In the UK, it is now a serious, criminal offence for a man on a country walk to pee behind a hedge. (Presumably, the Government has hired 100,000 snoops to hang around the countryside looking out for urinating walkers. Maybe they are using satellite technology.) And what is quite alarming is that everyone accepts most of what is happening. If the Government announced that it was planning to put sell-by-dates on loo rolls, and that it would be a criminal offence to sell, buy or own an out-of-date loo roll, there would be some tutting and possibly a little light sniggering but most people would simply shrug and accept it.

We live in a world of fines, licences and rules and these affect companies as much as individuals. The average business in the UK now spends £7,000 a year on fines. The most common penalties are for health and safety failings, late payment of taxes and fines from the Information Commissioner's Office.

Banks now routinely refuse to accept perfectly valid cheques, and direct debit instructions are ignored if a bank staff member wants to be annoying. None of this is happening accidental. It's all part of a concerted effort to force us to do all our banking online.

Righteousness is everywhere.

And every day, in every way, the customer's patience is tried.

Things that used to be routine (booking a ticket for a train) or renewing an insurance policy can take thirty minutes or more.

The rules, the cameras, the endless questionnaires, the implicit threats, the searches, the screening and the fines are not just a way of taking away our freedom but also a way to remind us that they can screw with us as much as they like, whenever they like, because most people will put up with the restrictions; and most of them do so, I'm afraid, because they mistakenly believe that in doing so they are exchanging their freedom for some security and a safer, better world.

What a pity that Sunday is no longer a special day of rest. Whether we go to church or not we need a day that is different. I can remember when Sundays were considered special and (literally) sacrosanct).

Governments should close down television stations and shut the internet so that people can have a little time to learn how to amuse themselves, to talk, to play music, to read and to make things.

Who knows, maybe some people would find the time to think a little.

John Buchan, the author of 'The Thirty Nine Steps', met T.E.Lawrence a short time before Lawrence's death.

Afterwards Buchan said to his wife that he thought T.E.L. (aka Lawrence of Arabia) was ready to return to a life of action and power.

Buchan's wife, Lady Tweedsmuir disagreed. 'He's looking at the world as God must look at it,' she said. 'And a man cannot do that and live.'

A few weeks later, Lawrence of Arabia was killed in a motorcycle accident.

Governments behave in very strange ways.

Here's an example.

In the year 2000, the Centers for Disease Control in the US asked Congress if they could find an extra $15 million to add to the CDC budget.

What did they want the money for?

Well, the CDC claimed that for $15 million they could wipe out syphilis from the US by 2005. Syphilis is a disease which runs in cycles, and in the year 2000 it was close to the critical point where it could be eradicated. The CDC wanted the extra money for the final push – a programme of offering free diagnoses and free treatment with penicillin.

Congress said 'No'. They said they couldn't find $15 million to wipe out a massively important disease.

Why?

Well, the simple answer is that health care has become massively politicised (largely because of the success that the AIDS movement had in managing to pressurise politicians, journalists and others to promote their interests and provide them with money) with the result that whoever shouts loudest gets the grant. Syphilis is a sexually transmitted disease which, in America, affects very poor African Americans – people who have very little clout with Congress (or had very little clout in the year 2000). In a world where $15 million is regarded as a rounding error by American politicians, it is shocking that Congress did not take note of this opportunity.

The fact is that health care everywhere is dominated by drug companies and pressure groups (often the same thing in practice) and there are lobby groups everywhere. There are even campaigners fighting for free access to infertility treatment for same sex couples.

And the result, of course, is that there was no money left for eradicating syphilis.

Antoinette has to take a drug called tamoxifen every day because she has hormone dependent breast cancer. We're having a devil of a job to obtain this essential, prescribed drug. (This has not been helped by the fact that one pharmacy, the one attached to our GP, refuses to obtain the drug at all because, although it is a commonly prescribed drug, obtaining it is 'a lot of trouble'.)

We have been repeatedly told (and this is the 'official' story) that it's difficult to get hold of the drug because there is, apparently, a nationwide shortage. Naturally, folk are blaming Brexit which is used by all political parties, all civil servants and all parts of the establishment as a weapon with which to beat the electorate for having dared to vote to take their country out of the European Union.

In this instance, the claim is particularly strange and indefensible because the box that the tamoxifen comes in says that the drug is made by a company in Leeds, Yorkshire. And that's really odd because I always thought Yorkshire was in England.

'There has never been a person in an old people's home that hasn't looked around dubiously at the other inhabitants. They are the old ones, they are the club that no one wants to join. But we are never old to ourselves. That is because at close of day the ship we sail in is the soul, not the body.' – Sebastian Barry

Most people don't have the attention span to deal with books. A recent study showed that 64% of Britons say they stop reading a book if the first few words don't catch their attention. So, if you got this far, you are clearly very special. But I knew that anyway.

'But here again, why will I thus entangle
Myself with metaphysics? None can hate
So much as I do any kind of wrangle;
And yet, such is my folly, or my fate,
I always knock my head against some angle
About the present, past or future state.'
Lord Byron
   (These lines are taken from the end of 'Don Juan' and at first I omitted the last two lines which seemed irrelevant for my purpose. But, on reflection, I find I must include them for they contain the best rhyme ever written by a poet. Here are the two final lines of Don Juan: 'Yet I wish well to Trojan and to Tyrian, For I was bred a moderate Presbyterian.' How can anyone not like a poet with such a delightful and absurd sense of self-mocking humour? The final rhyme appears to have been written by W.S.Gilbert. But it wasn't. It's pure Byron.)

Ageism which borders on contempt for older citizens is more widespread than most people realise. You only really get to notice how deeply rooted the ageism is until it hits you in the face like a wet mackerel. I can still remember visiting a highly esteemed dentist when I was in my mid 60s and being told that there wasn't any point in bothering to do anything to my teeth because I wouldn't be using them much longer. Since I was not obviously ailing or frail I thought this tactless and unprofessional.

'I was hoping to get a few more years value out of them,' I muttered.

He shrugged, turned away and told me to make another appointment for six months' time. I told him I wasn't sure I'd still be here then. And found another dentist who seemed quite a decent fellow and then promptly took early retirement.

I haven't been to the dentist since I tried a replacement for the decent one who retired. The replacement dentist took out a wisdom tooth which he broke. He had to dig the tooth out of my jaw in pieces. It was a distinctly unpleasant and exhausting procedure. Afterwards I developed a dry socket and then the socket became infected. I thought I might die during the extraction and I thought I might die afterwards when I needed to have the infection treated. It was all very uncomfortable and the problem was exacerbated by the fact that dentists routinely give very short courses of treatment for infections.

I've decided to clean my teeth regularly, use interdental brushes and hope for the best.

We apologise for any inconvenience.'
Sign outside gent's loo, closed for repairs, on the railway station at Weston-super-Mare, England

Ruthless ambition isn't a new phenomenon, of course. But I suspect that there are more ruthlessly ambitious people around these days than there ever were before. And I suspect too that they are willing to go further, and be more ruthless.

A good few years ago, Antoinette had an idea for a thriller which I thought particularly good. The idea was that a journalist working on a newspaper became famous by reporting on a series of murders. His in-depth assessments and apparent insider knowledge enabled him to stay ahead of the competition. He always seemed to have the details of the murders before any other reporters.

In the end it turns out that the reporter is the killer – and that he'd murdered people solely so that he could become a famous and successful journalist.

I played with the idea for years but never got round to writing it.

And then reality caught up with me.

A reporter called Vlado Taneski, who worked on a newspaper in Macedonia, wrote about the murder of a 61-year-old woman. The body had been dismembered, put into a plastic bag and dumped on a rubbish site. Taneski impressed his editor by managing to put more detail into the story than reporters working for other newspapers. Two men were convicted of the murder, and Taneski wrote a report from the courtroom.

Then another woman was murdered and again her dismembered body was found on a rubbish dump. Once more, Taneski wrote the story.

A few months later, a third woman was murdered and this time Taneski made a mistake with his story. Having suggested that the murders were the work of a serial killer, the reporter wrote that the body had been tied up with a piece of phone cable 'with which the woman had clearly been previously strangled'.

No other reporter knew of the phone cable. The police hadn't released that piece of information.

And in due course the police arrested Taneski. His DNA connected him to the murders. And all three women, who had all been cleaners, had known Taneski's mother.

The killer was never taken to court because he was found dead in jail. The police said it was suicide.

Who was it who said that truth is stranger than fiction?

Reading Arthur Lubow's marvellous biography of Richard Harding Davis ('The Reporter who would be king') I found this wonderful sentence: 'It's a well-established rule of commercial fiction that the authors who succeed are not those who tailor their work to the public taste, but those who, writing to please themselves, happily find that their own preferences are shared by the millions.'

Davis who worked in America at what I still think of as the 'turn of the century' (the end of the 19th century and the beginning of the

20th century) was the first celebrity journalist, though he also wrote books and plays.

We tend to think of instant celebrity as a modern phenomenon; here today and gone tomorrow. Andy Warhol's fifteen minutes of fame may have been an exaggeration but not by much. Reality TV stars swoosh into show business and whoosh out again before anyone has learnt to put names to the faces. Davis lasted much longer than fifteen minutes, remaining a star throughout his life. But within days of his demise he was forgotten. He was the first human shooting star. You'd be hard pressed to find a book by him in a second-hand bookshop today and I doubt if any of his plays has been produced for a century or more. But during his lifetime he was one of the most recognisable and saleable commodities in the United States. And most celebrities would be very happy with that. Most modern media stars would probably agree that there's not much point in being a celebrity when you're dead.

Company bosses, politicians and celebrities who get themselves into a public relations tangle should remember Lemmy Kilmister of the rock group Motorhead.

A few years ago newspapers everywhere ran an apology demanded by Lemmy's lawyers.

The news stories were all much like this: 'Lawyers for Motorhead star Lemmy have complained about a story entitled 'Motorhead Lemmy in bondage romp' which told how the 55-year-old Motorhead rocker handcuffed his lover to the bed for a three day sex and bondage session. Mr Lemmy's solicitors would like us to point out that it was not three days and she was not handcuffed to the bed. It was seven days and she was hung from the ceiling. We apologise unreservedly to Mr Lemmy for any damage caused to his reputation.'

I have never come across a better example of Imperial thoughtlessness than the fact that when they ruled India, the British introduced a new Enfield rifle which used greased cartridges. The cartridges were smeared with the fat of cows and pigs thus, very nicely outraging the feelings of both Hindus, to whom the cow was sacred, and Muslims, to whom the pig was unclean. This thoughtlessness helped spark the fire that became the Indian Mutiny.

I try to avoid obituaries. If I see that someone has died at a younger age than I am then I tend to think more than ever that I must be on borrowed time.

However old you are, you still have to plan for the future in a positive way – or you are merely marking time, filling in the hours until the final whistle. We need plans and ambitions but most of us feel we need to be flexible enough to allow for unforeseen events without causing crises. Some courageous souls, however, can simply ignore reality and carry on regardless.

When he was seriously ill (he had laryngeal cancer and had suffered a number of heart attacks), Evan Hunter the novelist (who was also known as Ed McBain) announced that he was beginning a new series of books about a new character. He declared that he was planning 26 books and that each book would start with a title starting with a different letter of the alphabet. The first book in the series was entitled 'Alice in Jeopardy'. Sadly, that was the only book in the series. But you have to give the man full marks for courage and for ambition.

Nothing that happens has any influence unless it is reported, and so the corrupt and total conversion of the media into a method of spreading propaganda has destroyed the free press and with it our freedom and our liberty.

Nothing that has happened in my lifetime has shocked me more, or frightened me more, than the willing subjugation of the media to the whims and fancies of the spring-pullers. The BBC in particular has betrayed its founder's hopes and promises with a steely determination and has become little more than a propaganda vehicle.

Not all that long ago journalism was a profession where

honourable, honest journalists could exist and even thrive. It's true, of course, that newspapers and television companies were invariably controlled by companies with policies to pursue and political allegiances to promote and defend, but there were still pockets of truth available for discerning readers and viewers.

That has changed.

Deception and propaganda have infiltrated the news. Kickbacks, bribery and protection rackets are commonplace. Even weather forecasts are bent.

The result is that the mainstream media manages to combine toxic and determined ignorance with elitism and self-righteousness. Nations, industries, professions are run by the corrupt and protected from exposure by the corrupt.

Most newspapers and magazines are now written and edited by impoverished 20-year-olds who have been hired because they are cheap, who have not yet grown out of their adolescent naivety, who are always happy to put prejudice before facts, who do not have the courage, integrity or intelligence to question what they are told to write by politicians, lobbyists and advertisers, and whose most notable qualities are a sense of entitlement and a deep-rooted resentment. This is, of course, is the same for the broadcast media – only more so.

Any honest print or broadcast journalist would be fired in minutes if he said or wrote anything which went against official policy. What a sad state of affairs that is.

The laziness of millennials and members of the Z generation is legendary. I recently saw a company advertising a service whereby they would send two slices of bread and a pot of butter by mail order to their customers. And they would do this each day. Those customers who paid extra could also have a small pot of marmalade sent to them. The unique selling point seemed to be that this would save the busy millennial the job of preparing their own breakfast. The ingredients would be delivered to their door every day of the week.

Mindfulness has been a popular trend for a long time now but as a concept it has been around for centuries.

It has become particularly popular among millennials – some of whom probably think they invented it. (Or that it was invented for them.)

But here's the joke.

The principle of mindfulness is that you should enjoy the moment. You should be totally aware of what is going on around you.

So how do millennials practise their mindfulness?

They spend every waking moment taking selfies so that they can preserve the moment they are about to just miss, and then examine the moment more closely at some future time which will never come. It is reported from New York that the average young family of four takes five thousand photos a year. The accumulation of photos is so out of control that it has become fashionable to hire a photo manager, at a hundred and twenty five dollars an hour, to sort out the huge store of pictures which accumulate. The aim, apparently, is to cut the photos down to no more than twelve hundred 'keepers' on the inevitable iPhone, with a couple of hundred for a digital album and twelve to fifteen to have printed to hang on the wall. After ten years, the average family will still have 12,000 'special' photos in their album.

When do the selfie takers find time to look at all their pictures?

And when they aren't taking interminable selfies, the millennials are busy recording their trivial, everyday exploits, in great detail, on their social media accounts.

The principles of mindfulness are that you look, observe, feel, experience and enjoy.

Still, millennials will, I suspect, continue to do things their own way.

I overheard two millennials in a café yesterday. They may have been Gen Zers. It's difficult to tell. They all look and behave as if they were about twelve-years-old.

'My boss is terrible,' said one. 'He keeps trying to tell me what to do!'

'You should complain,' said the other. 'I'm sure he isn't allowed to do that.'

And I heard another millennial talking about climate change, energy and the planet.

'I don't know why they burn coal or diesel or gas any more. And I don't know why they're putting up these horrid windmills and solar panels. Electricity is so much cleaner. It just comes out of the socket and there's no mess.'

Bless them. They're quite sweet in a bunny rabbit sort of way, aren't they?

Their theme tune should be 'We want the world and we want it now' sung by Jim Morrison and the Doors.

Meanwhile, millennials and the Z generation aren't too keen on work. They prefer to stay at home. If work is entirely unavoidable (and they have failed to succeed as internet influencers) they prefer to take on undemanding unemployment with their government, their local council or, best of all, the BBC.

And the next generation (known as the Alphas) are even worse. Most of them spend at least three hours a day looking at their smart phones (and don't have time for boring stuff such as reading, writing and arithmetic). In the US, girls aged between eight and 12 spend $40 million a month on beauty products and are the largest growth market for cosmetics.

I sometimes feel as though I am an alien.

Or, maybe, a human on an alien planet.

I saw an advertisement for a GP to work on a small Scottish island. I wish I were a few decades younger. One of my serious regrets is that I never really worked as a lone GP. When I started as a GP, I had my own practice and my own surgery but shared on-call duties with other GPs, working at other premises. The rules in those days forbad doctors from working alone.

Looking after a community on an island is my idea of a perfect GP practice.

But whoever is advertising for a young doctor to take on the job is obviously having difficulty in finding a candidate, for the job offers £150,000 a year and a fine selection of perks. Maybe the lucky candidate who gets the job will build their own house on the island in the style of Henry David Thoreau.

It has seemed to me for quite a while that Britons have been getting increasingly miserable. Everywhere you go there are long faces and moans. Irritability is commoner than smiles. I cannot remember seeing so much misery.

And now there is evidence proving that the observation is accurate.

A neuroscience foundation has done research showing that the UK is the second most miserable country in the world – behind only Uzbekistan. The survey, which involved 419,175 individuals in 71 countries showed that other English speaking countries are also doing badly, with Australia, New Zealand and Ireland down there with the most miserable countries on the planet. As far as mental health is concerned, the UK is eight places behind Yemen and 12 places behind Ukraine. An astonishing 35% of Britons admit that they are either 'distressed' or 'struggling'.

And evidence from elsewhere confirms these findings. A paper in The Lancet reported that 1.8 million people in the UK are currently awaiting mental health treatment. And problems seem to be exacerbated when children are given smart phones at an early age.

The happiest country in the world is the Dominican Republic with Sri Lanka second and Tanzania third.

The phrase 'Nice to see you again, sir!' (or 'Nice to see you again, madam!') has to be the cheesiest greeting ever used by hotel and restaurant staff.

The idea, of course, is to make the guest feel welcome, and the doorman (or whoever) who utters this banality knows that he can't go wrong.

If the guest has been to the establishment before he'll be thrilled to be recognised. If he hasn't visited before then he'll just assume that the greeter recognises him from somewhere else. It's a win-win for the doorman. And it's cheesy. And tacky. And it has, of course, devalued what, a long time ago, used to be a genuine greeting.

And have you noticed that people don't have holidays anymore? They go on annual leave – which I always thought of as a military affectation.

In cafes, pubs and shops the staff respond to any request with the promise that it is 'no problem', though they never explain why doing their job should or could be a problem and the phrase rather implies that they're somehow condescending to do you a favour. And if you buy something, the salesperson will, after expressing admiration for your choice and taste (as in 'Oh, I noticed that and thought I might buy one for myself') instruct you to 'enjoy'!

We have fed nuts to the squirrels in our garden for years. We feed them walnuts, hazelnuts and peanuts (all in the shells). Recently we noticed that a rat was joining in and, as rats are want to do, he was fighting the squirrels and attacking the birds (the crows are particularly fond of the peanuts in their shells) so we decided that instead of putting the nuts on the ground, as we had been doing, we would put them on the bird table, which has a rather nice tiled roof held up by pillars. Rats, of course, cannot deal with an overhang – which is why farmers used to store their corn in barns resting on saddle stones. The bird feeders all hang from the sides of the table from cup hooks (which I'm proud to say I added myself).

The problem has been that when putting nuts onto the table, several of them, particularly the walnuts, would roll off onto the grass and need picking up and replacing. So I used panel pins to nail narrow strips of the wood to the openings between the pillars. I decided that this is probably the perfect definition of an 'odd job'.

And I am proud to regard myself as an odd job man.

I am tired of the barrage of emails I receive every time I order something.

For example, look at this series of messages I received for a small parcel being handled by a delivery company called Yodel. On the 4th December, I ordered a humane mousetrap because we had a mouse in the pantry and the nearest shop, which is ten miles away, only sells mouse traps which don't work. On the 6 Dec at 9.19 pm I received a message giving me a tracking number for the order. I was given a delivery date of 8th December. I am grown up and experienced in these matters and did not take this seriously. Here are the messages which I subsequently received.

6 Dec
9.49 pm 'Your parcel has arrived at your delivery depot'
6 Dec
10.10 pm 'Your parcel collection has been booked (London).'
7 Dec
12.00 am 'We are expecting your parcel from your sender. We will provide updates here once we receive it (London)'
7 Dec
10.04 am 'Your driver is coming to collect your parcel (London)'
7 Dec
11.53 am 'We've collected your parcel (London).'
7 Dec
4.13 pm 'Your parcel has arrived in our depot (London).'
7 Dec
9.42 pm 'We have your parcel. Please check back for updates (London).'
8 Dec
10.53 am 'Your parcel is at our national hub (Wednesbury).'
9 Dec
4.24 am 'Your parcel has arrived at your delivery depot (Yeovil).'
9 Dec
5.22 am 'Your parcel has arrived at your delivery depot (Yeovil).'
9 Dec
8.39 am 'Your parcel has arrived at your delivery depot (Yeovil).'
9 Dec
12.14 pm 'Your parcel has arrived at your delivery depot (Yeovil).'

(At this point it occurred to me that it might be a good idea if the Yodel people left their computer terminals, tossed the packet into the back of a van and set about delivering it.)

10 Dec
7.55 am 'Your parcel has arrived at your delivery depot (Yeovil).'
10th Dec
8.30 am 'We have your parcel. Please check back for updates.'

10 Dec
8.30 am 'Your parcel is with one of our drivers for delivery.'
10 Dec
11.03 'Your parcel has been delivered to a safe place.'

The parcel was actually placed on the step outside our side gate. No one rang the bell. Naturally, we also received subsequent emails both from Yodel and the sender to let us know the good news and to ask us to rate the delivery. I gave the delivery driver full marks. Whenever a parcel arrives I always give the delivery driver full marks.

Like everyone, I receive far too many nuisance calls on my mobile phone. Since very few people have the number, I always answer when it rings since there's a fair assumption that the call is important. However, despite the number being ex-directory, I still receive the usual garbage (usually from somewhere on the other side of the globe). This morning I received such a call while I was in the bank. I answered the call straight away (thinking it might be Antoinette) and a man, speaking broken almost incomprehensible English, started to tell me what he was selling. 'I'm sorry,' I said (since I am English I invariably apologise even when I haven't done anything wrong), 'but I'm in the middle of an operation.' The man apologised profusely and hung up. This seems to me to be the quickest way to deal with one of these calls. If a caller doesn't hang up the next time I try this I'll add a little colour. 'Look out for that bleeding, sister. And someone take this phone off me while I sew up this heart.'

Some time ago, Antoinette and I bought a double gravestone plot in a nearby cemetery. It's a decent sort of position, next to a wildlife reserve. At some point we will, I suppose, have to decide what we want on our two-for-one gravestone.

The best ever gravestone inscription is without a doubt the one on Mel Blanc's grave. Blanc was the voice of Bugs Bunny and the message on his gravestone is: 'That's all folks!'

I'll be happy to have 'He made people think' on mine (I'll accept

'He tried to make people think') though I have no doubt the establishment would prefer something libellous and dismissive. This is, I suppose, a variation on Kenneth Tynan's more wordy thought that he 'enjoyed exposing people to ideas and experiences that helped people reassess the values by which they lived'.

Political correctness means that we have lost a huge chunk of our humour.

In a patriotic, World War II tune, music hall and film star George Formby sang about Mr Wu, his famous Chinese laundry man. The song is entitled 'Mr Wu's an air raid warden now' and in between the usual frantic strumming contains the line: 'If you've got a chink in your window you'll have another one at your door.'

The BBC was happy to play the song during World War II but collective BBC executives would have fits if anyone considered playing it these days.

I once put together a selection of eight gramophone records for the BBC Desert Island Discs programme. All the records, including 'Mr Wu's an air raid warden now' and 'Je t'aime' with Serge Gainsbourg and Jane Birkin, had been banned. But, not surprisingly, the BBC never invited me onto their programme and so the list remained of theoretical interest only.

The list of records which have been banned by the BBC seems to be endless and sometimes quite inexplicable. The banned records include 'Danny Boy', 'The Deck of Cards', 'Charlie Brown', 'Back in the USSR', 'The Blue Danube', 'A Day in the Life', 'Don't let's be Beastly to the Germans', 'Give Peace a Chance', 'Greensleeves', 'I am the Walrus', 'I'll be Home for Christmas', `Waterloo', 'Tell Laura I Love Her', 'Stranger in Paradise', 'Space Oddity' and, curiously, a record called 'Radio Times' recorded by the BBC Dance Orchestra.

The sad fact is that the censors are everywhere these days. Whole series of books have been rewritten by cautious publishers in order to remove all words, phrases, sentences or jokes which might cause offence to someone. There is always someone somewhere who is prepared to take offence and make a fuss.

The woke control so much of the world these days that they have done their best to wreck literature and films. The last James Bond film was the nearest thing I've seen to a corporate suicide note. And the woke are mercilessly unforgiving.

Even the original version of the seemingly harmless film Mary Poppins (made 60 years ago) has been declared unsuitable for children who are not accompanied by an adult. The problem, apparently, is that the film contains the word 'hottentot', the name which was once used by Europeans to refer to a group of nomads in South Africa. I understand that the name is now considered unacceptable and has been replaced by the word 'khoekhoe' which is more difficult to pronounce and more difficult to spell and therefore much more acceptable. The British Board of Film Classification apparently fears that unaccompanied children will be permanently damaged whereas children who have an adult with them will be safe. I'd bet that 99% of all those watching the film won't have the faintest idea what the word 'hottentot' means. I assume that my use of the word in this paragraph means that this book will be declared unsuitable for young children to read unless they are unaccompanied by at least one adult. This book will be given an X certificate and, if it ever gets into a bookshop (which is extremely unlikely since when the two words 'Vernon' and 'Coleman' are placed in conjunction on a book cover then the contents will be considered too scary for public consumption), it will be placed in a small room at the back, wrapped in plastic or brown paper and stored with other revolutionary volumes.

My contract for the film of my novel Mrs Caldicot's Cabbage War allowed me to write a theatrical play based on the book, and so I did. When I'd finished writing the play, I sent off copies to most of the big, professional theatres. One or two sent me nice letters, praising the play (one said it reminded him of Oscar Wilde) but confessing that since it seemed to deal with old, white people it wasn't anything they'd want to put on. What really surprised me, however, was that although I enclosed stamped self-addressed envelopes with the copies of the play, most of the theatres just kept the stamps and threw away the plays. Not even the National Theatre bothered to stuff the play in its envelope and post it back to me. Book publishers and agents are the same these days. They presumably steam the stamps off the envelopes and reuse them.

Undaunted I decided to make the play available to amateur dramatic societies.

The only way to interest a professional theatre in putting on the play, would be to identify myself as a black, 20-year-old female and to change Mrs Caldicot, (an old aged pensioner, and the entire troupe of newly independent old aged pensioners whom she looks after) into the teenage members of a Black Lives Matter group of Zionist activists fighting a war against imperialist domination and demanding more extensive benefits for black teenage mothers. If I include a diatribe against the British Empire, and a thoroughly vicious attack on white males who are over 40 and not renowned sports stars, I should be home and dry with a season at the National Theatre a certainty.

When I wrote the play, I thought it would be fun for amateur dramatic societies to perform it without the big fees that are usually charged. So I announced that the play could be performed free by amateur dramatic societies anywhere in the world. I thought that the small amounts of money I made from selling the printed versions of the play would at least provide me with some recompense.

(I receive around $1.89 for each copy of the play – according to whether it is purchased from a bookshop or bought directly from the website. If a production requires 20 copies of the play, for cast and crew, that would give me an income of under $40 for a production – compared to a fee many times that which would be normally charged for a performance. And some amateur societies perform to many hundreds of customers who sometimes pay quite high prices for tickets.)

Sadly, I suspected that some societies were buying one copy of the play and then copying it. Moreover, since I wasn't charging a full commercial rate, drama companies felt they could do as they liked and were changing the script according to the egotistical demands of individual actors without bothering to ask permission. ('I'd like a bigger part so I'll write in a few lines for myself.')

The trouble, of course, is that people have learned not to value things which they don't pay for, and respect for other people's work is thought of as being very 1950s. There are many people who now regard copyright as theft. Big sites such as YouTube which allow films and broadcasts to be stolen and 'published' are very much to blame. Naturally, the people who put stolen items on YouTube do then make a great deal of money by monetising their channels and claiming the advertising income from YouTube. And, of course, YouTube makes a ton of money this way. Copyright theft is one of the few types of theft which now seems to be approved by the authorities.

We were preparing to go out for a drive in the Bentley when a sizeable crowd of walkers, all strangers, collected on the road outside our gates. They were all admiring the car. I started the engine, took off the handbrake and allowed the car to roll forwards down to the road. I then made the mistake of putting my foot on the accelerator before I'd moved the gear lever out of neutral and into drive. Naturally, the engine howled in protest. Naturally, I've never done that before and I doubt if I'll do it again. I apologised to the Bentley which was very good about it and remained unperturbed.

I miss having a small, annual pocket diary. On the 31st December each year, I would put my brand new leather backed diary next to my old, worn diary and transfer birthdays and other significant dates from the latter to the former. I would write in any important events (such as the summer's Test Matches, examination dates and so on) and then I would start to browse through the fun pages at the back and the front. The diary publishers always included a list of metric and imperial measures so that readers could check up on the number of perches in a rood or the length of a chain. There was a comparison table giving shoe and skirt sizes for Europe, the UK and the USA, and there was a table to enable the reader to convert metres into yards and degrees Fahrenheit into degrees Centigrade. There would usually be a table of paper sizes and, best of all, a couple of pages giving the distances in miles between cities around the world. The distance between London and Beijing and London and Reykjavik would be there for you in an instant. And the same table would always have the time differences too. If stuck at a railway station, you could study your diary for hours. And the battery never went flat.

I drove Antoinette to the local pharmacy to pick up her regular prescription. I managed to park right outside the shop and stayed with the car. When the pharmacist had given Antoinette her medicine, he saw the Bentley parked outside. He escorted her to the shop door, opened the door for her and bowed. I wonder if he would have done that if we'd turned up in our truck.

When she was 83-years-old, Doris Day, the film star and singer, was invited to accept a Lifetime Achievement award at the Oscars. But two days before the ceremony one of Ms Day's 17 dogs was hit by a car, Naturally, Ms Day insisted on remaining with the injured animal. When the legendary star didn't turn up to accept the award, the Academy withdrew the offer and didn't repeat it. I lost what little respect I had for the Oscars when I heard that.

(I too was once offered an award which I couldn't collect. And my award was withdrawn and given to someone else. I cannot for the life of me remember what the award was called but I am pretty sure it wasn't an Oscar.)

'I feel that there is something deeply, deeply wrong which nothing but some great strong new force can set right.'
Sir Arthur Conan Doyle

Recycling is nothing more than a compliance training exercise. As an exercise in salvaging useable materials, it is a waste of time and energy. Actually, it's worse than a waste because the cost of collecting the so-called recyclables, and then sending them off to dumps in far parts of the world, is massive and the cost to the environment is enormous.

I cannot help remembering that when I was a boy, the milkman used to call every day and collect our empty milk bottles. Moreover, the local shop used to give a couple of pennies back on every pop bottle that was returned. Bottles were well looked after and always returned to be reused because they were worth money.

Today, buying and running an old Bentley is the purest form of recycling. If or when old Bentleys are beyond restoration, they are carefully taken to pieces and the bits and pieces are sold to help restore other old Bentleys. So, for example, when I needed a new radiator, I bought a restored radiator. And the garage sent the broken radiator to a specialist who will mend it and sell it to someone else.

In the old days, if an inaccurate, libellous or simply spiteful review was published, an author could write to the editor and expect a reasonable correction or protest to be published. The writer had a defence and a voice. But in the internet in general this isn't possible. The author has no freedom or right to defend him or herself, and the parameters for reviewing have changed dramatically.

Reviewers used to look to see how well the author of a book had achieved his aim and how other readers might react to the book. ('Will they enjoy it? Will readers find it useful?) That's all changed and online reviews of whatever it is tend to be very personal. Anonymous spite can do great damage to an author or a book or a play or a film or a café.

One reader gave each of my first two diaries a single star and then put the third book on his or her wish-list. Why would anyone do that? A reviewer who gave one of my polemics a single star complained that the book contained 'opinions'. Someone called Jennie dismissed my book 'Mrs Caldicot's Cabbage War' with the words 'Don't waiste your money' (sic) on 21.10.14 and then, on the same day, wrote a review of the sequel 'Mrs Caldicot's Knickerbocker Glory' in which she said: 'What a load of rubbish. Wish I had not waisted my money!!!' (sic) Did she really buy the second book, or did she just dislike the first so much that she felt a need to double up on the abuse? My admittedly quirky and very personal book 'Secrets of Paris' received rave reviews from magazine reviewers but when it was published online, it was slammed because it didn't contain details of museums and hotels. I spent many months researching my book 'Dr Bullock's Annals', which is a novel about the life of a Victorian doctor. Every line in it is absolutely accurate. Inevitably, the first review was from someone who claimed that the book was unrealistic and gave it one star. One reader complained about my book 'The Awakening of Dr Amelia Leighton' because, he claimed, nothing happened. It is true that there are no murders or car chases but the novel is about a young woman doctor whose entire life changes. She begins the book as an unsatisfied GP working in a soulless city practice and, after personal and professional trials and tribulations, ends up living in a country cottage and working in a country practice. It is a story about enlightenment and liberation – with lots of strange and fun things occurring on the way. My book on vaccines and vaccination received a mass of one star reviews from people who admitted (or sometimes boasted) that they hadn't bothered to read the book, or even look at it. (Some of those were subsequently removed.)

My favourite ever review was from someone who wrote: 'I find it difficult to comment on this because I know nothing about this subject and haven't read the book which I bought for someone else.' And then gave the book one star.

Actually, reviews are commonly written by people who haven't ever seen a copy of the book they are reviewing. Their review is merely a way of sharing an opinion. A good number of the reviews I get online are from people who don't bother to write a review but just slam a one star rating on the book. It's usually an ad hominem criticism done out of spite rather than anything else. When you've spent years studying a subject and working on a book such reviews can be a trifle irritating.

I write many different types of book and this can cause me huge problems. Reviews along the lines of 'I love his Bilbury books but there was nothing about Bilbury in this book about high blood pressure (or whatever)' are commonplace and inevitably accompanied by a one star review.

Quite often an author or film maker is hammered for something that wasn't his or her fault. For example, consider this review which appeared (with a one star review) of my book on 'High Blood Pressure' (and which, because one star reviews are given more authority than five star reviews, had a significant impact on my income from the book): 'My paperback book came in a bubble envelope and it was very crinkled, bent up and hard to read. Next time may I suggest you put a thin paperback in something much sturdier for mailing. Thank you.'

Since I don't put the books in envelopes and Amazon use cardboard envelopes, I can only assume that the buyer purchased their book from a third party seller who was flogging a second-hand book. So, as a bonus, I earned nothing from the sale.

I wrote a book entitled 'Vernon Coleman's English Heroes'. One of the earliest reviewers attacked the book because I included Lord Byron in my list of 100 great Englishmen. The reviewer didn't like Byron's sexual history. I didn't include him in the book because of his sexual history but because of his poetry. Then someone complained about Churchill being on the list because he'd encouraged the killing of many Germans. And another reviewer complained that Dickens and Shakespeare shouldn't have been included because some of their writing might be considered anti-semitic. How could you produce a list of 100 great Englishmen without including Dickens, Shakespeare, Churchill and Byron on the list? Claiming that someone shouldn't be on the list because you don't like their personal habits is childish.

And then there are the crazy reviews. So, for example, there is a two star review of one of my books which reads: 'I decided not to buy this book but to buy another book instead.' That was the first review the book received and it killed the sales stone dead.

When I complained about a particularly libellous review of one of my books which had appeared, the site responded by banning me from ever posting any more reviews of my own And they deleted all my own reviews on that site. Read that again. I still don't quite understand it. I'm training myself not to care but it isn't easy.

I'm by no means the only author to be puzzled by strange reviewers. John Grisham, the hugely successful American novelist (whose first book was self-published) wrote: 'Reviewers with too much time on their hands love nit-picking and finding tiny, inconsequential errors in novels.' Grisham pre-empted further criticisms with this note at the end of his book 'The Last Juror': 'I took great liberty with a few of the laws that existed in Mississippi in the 1970s. The ones I mistreated in this book have now been amended and improved. I misused them to move my story along. I do this all the time and never feel guilty about it, since I can always disclaim things on this page. If you spot these mistakes, please don't write me a letter. I acknowledge my mistakes. They were intentional.'

Finally, there is a wonderful quote from drama critic Ken Tynan: 'A critic is someone who knows the way, but cannot drive the car.'

The mass of people have, it seems, willingly handed over their independence, both of thought and physical being, to the State. Most people want more public services and want their Government to take on more power and responsibilities. Most people want higher taxes. (Though, it should be pointed out, most people who want higher taxes do not pay any tax because they are, for one reason or another, unemployed. Others who want more Government expenditure are employees of the State with a vested interest in maintaining the size and power of the State.)

This transfer of power and responsibility governs every aspect of our lives.

So, for example, whenever the weather is inclement, Government propagandists swing into action with advice about keeping warm, avoiding unnecessary travel and wearing coats, scarves and gloves if it is necessary to venture out of doors. (Curiously, hats do not figure in the advice.)

And if the weather is warm, there is advice about not sitting in the sun for too long and remembering to drink lots of fluids. We are all treated like slightly backward four-year-olds. And most people seem to find this reassuring and even comforting.

Members of the Z generation and millennials are famous (or infamous) for their diva –type behaviour. But there is something of the prima donna (or the diva) in all of us and from time to time we are all entitled to stamp a foot (whether it be attired in a delicate ballet shoe or wrapped in a stout, nailed walking shoe), stand your ground and allow yourself to wander north from eccentricity into the wilder realms of tempestuous unreasonableness.

Rest assured, however, that however diva-ish you may become it is extremely unlikely that you will reach the heights of opera singers who are justifiably famous for their little ways. Rock bands demanding snooker tables backstage and huge bowls of Smarties with all the brown ones removed are nothing compared with opera singers. (To be fair, if I had to go out onto a stage in front of several thousand axe wielding critics and rely entirely on absurd vocal gymnastics to keep the crowd quiet, I would out-tantrum them all.)

In the world of opera it is generally accepted that the most absurd behaviour is exhibited not by sopranos or basses but by tenors. Men who can wander around middle C are rare men indeed and in addition to being paid a fortune, they generally expect to be cossetted and to have their whims and fancies honoured and humoured. And theatre managers know what to expect.

For example, consider Franco Corelli, who was in his day one of the world's great tenors. His demand that he be fed steak tartare, garnished with raw garlic and lemon, before every performance was not particularly unusual but when he arrived in a country to be expected to be greeted at the local airport with much pazzazz. He once abandoned a whole season at the Paris Opera because there was no red carpet awaiting his arrival at Paris Charles de Gaulle airport. He just turned round, caught another plane and went home.

And when a performance began, there was no knowing what would happen. At the New York Met he once delayed his entrance in a performance of Don Carlos while he continued a row backstage with his wife (who was also his manager). Not surprisingly he did not like being heckled and when someone booed him during a performance of Il Trovatore in Naples, he left the stage, ran up three flights of stairs and physically attacked the heckler. When he and Boris Christoff fell out (who knows what over) the two used stage swords to try to kill each other. In 1961, when his co-star Birgit Nilsson held her top C for longer than he had, Corelli walked off stage. The manager found him in his dressing room screaming at the top of his voice. (And opera singers can scream loudly.) Corelli's wife was also screaming. And a dog was barking. And there was blood everywhere because Corelli had smashed his hand in his fury. To get his tenor back on stage, the manager suggested that Corelli get his own back in the third act when he and Ms Nilsson were due to embrace. 'Bite her ear,' suggested the manager in desperation. And so that's what he did. The wounded Ms Nilsson allegedly demanded that she be tested for rabies.

They don't make 'em like that anymore, more's the pity. Today, such behaviour would result in a torrent of lawsuits and a lifetime ban.

As I approach what I like to think of as the dreary, predictable foothills of middle age, I occasionally look back at the things I have learned. Here's one: whenever there is a choice (in private clubs and so on) I always vote against everything, for this is the only sure way in which we can combat cliques and fascism. Having said that, I should point out, perhaps, that although I have been a member of a number of clubs, there are only two clubs in London which are worth joining: the Drones' Club and the Diogenes Club and neither of them is open to new members. The Drones' Club, for boisterous young men, was invented by P.G.Wodehouse for Bertie Wooster and the Diogenes Club, for quiet, shy, antisocial gentlemen of mature years was invented by Arthur Conan-Doyle for Sherlock Holmes's brother Mycroft. Neither of these clubs actually exists, of course.

It used to be said that children should be seen but not heard. During the last few decades, a corollary to that saying has emerged; the rarely articulated but very modern feeling that the elderly should be neither seen nor heard. They should, so it seems, retire into obscurity and leave the business of life and living to younger folk. For their own (and everyone else's convenience) the elderly should live in special ghettoes called care homes and rest homes where they should integrate with one another, do a good deal of television watching, be grateful for what they receive and generally hide away from the real world and real life. Most important of all, they should accept that their lives are over and, as residents of God's waiting room, they should sit quietly in plastic covered chairs, take whatever tablets they are given, try not to smell too much or to make socially unacceptable noises, and make no attempt to interfere with the adults struggling to run the real world. The old-fashioned notion that the elderly should share their acquired knowledge and their experience for the benefit of the coming generations has been replaced by the notion that the elderly know nothing of value and that their experiences have been devalued by the pace of life. The next, logical step in this progression is, of course, the feeling that it makes good economic and social sense to help the elderly out of this world and into the next at the slightest provocation. The current enthusiasm for euthanasia and for encouraging the elderly to have Do Not Resuscitate scrawled on their medical notes is the end result.

We had a letter from the electricity grid to tell us that they would turn off our electricity for the day so that they could trim trees near to our overhead electricity power cables. With no electricity we would have no heating, no cooking, no light to read, no computers, nothing much but these days we grab each day and squeeze all the goodness out of it and we weren't going to let a little thing like no electricity get in the way of that philosophy. So we got up early enough to boil water for a couple of flasks, dressed, had hot drinks, climbed into the Bentley and went out for the day. It was one of the most fun days I've had for a long while. There was no sense of guilt that I should be doing something and we knew we had to be out all day. We stopped at the paper shop and bought a huge pile of newspapers, not because we wanted to read them but because we had run out of newspaper for lighting the fire, and then drove ten or so miles along the coast until we reached a small town that still had its electricity. We parked and then walked leisurely along the sea front. We went into an antique centre where I spent more time browsing among the books than I would normally allow and bought seven paperbacks that I didn't know that I wanted. At another slightly more up market shop which sold old stuff, we bought a beautiful vase that we didn't know we needed but definitely wanted. (Antoinette paints flowers and needs good jugs and vases in which to present them). We then went into a coffee shop where we sat without once looking at our watches or thinking of the things we had to do. I had taken the precaution of ripping the crosswords out of two of the newspapers we had bought so we completed those together. Then we retraced our steps, drove home and arrived there just as the electricity came back on again. We had done nothing of value, done nothing planned and achieved nothing but felt that we had squeezed the day so firmly that we'd got the pips out of it.

Twice in my life I have been investigated by the tax authorities. Before you jump to erroneous conclusions, I will add that on both occasions the inquiries ended with the tax authorities paying me quite large sums of money when, after lengthy enquiries, they eventually found that I had overpaid my taxes. On one occasion my accountant was at fault and excused his egregious errors by claiming that his firm was using out-of-date textbooks. (You will not be surprised to hear that I sacked him.)

There is a widespread misconception that if you get picked out by the tax people then you have probably done something wrong. Too many people believe the 'no smoke without fire' philosophy which is so beloved by gossips everywhere. That's quite wrong. In my case I was, on both occasions, the innocent victim picked out by people who reported me to the tax people simply in order to gain brownie points and to get the tax office off their own backs.

When I was young very few people would snitch on their friends, colleagues or neighbours. But today, all around the world, governments are encouraging their citizens to sneak on one another; to become part of an unofficial secret police force.

In Greece, for example, the Government has promised to pay cash payments of up to 3,000 euros to anyone who reports one or more tax evaders. The offer has been very successful, and in December 2023 it was reported that the Greek Government has received 136,287 reports since the offer was made.

There is, of course, much more money to be paid by sneaking in the USA. A whistleblower in America who provided the IRS with information was given a reward of $15.1 million.

All this is very sad for there is no doubt that the encouragement of snitching and sneaking creates suspicion and distrust. The world of social credit, as introduced in China, is well and truly here to stay.

The internet is, without doubt, the most damaging, destructive, dangerous and ultimately evil invention ever made. It is worse than the atomic bomb, cigarettes and plastic sandals.

The internet and social media could have encouraged a sense of community and helped people connect with one another. Instead, social media exists merely to isolate, to promote abuse and to encourage a sense of entitlement. I am, of course, commenting as an outsider since I am merely a professional victim of social media. People lie about me because I am banned from all social media and am not allowed to see what they have written, defend myself, correct mistakes or respond in any way. (I know that social media is awash with lies because kind friends show them to me.)

For several years now there have been several fake social media sites in my name. The irony, of course, is that I am banned by these sites (and only know about the fake sites because I've been told about them) but other people are allowed to use my name and image and to pretend to be me. I have made repeated complaints to the companies concerned but they simply ignore the protests.

Politicians who are abused online can insist that the social media companies remove libellous or threatening remarks. There is no such protection for those of us who are not well-paid public servants.

And social media is used as a weapon. A man who runs a few holiday cottages reported recently that when a boiler misbehaved in one of the cottages he owns, a holidaymaker stood before him, bristling and defiant, and said: 'Do you want to give me a refund or do you want to wait and read the review on Trip Advisor?'

Our decision to 'pick'n'mix' the repairs on our Bentley isn't unique. In a car magazine called 'Rolls Royce and Bentley driver' I read about an enthusiast who owned a 1961 Silver Cloud II (a similar model to our Bentley S) but who had not used his car for a while. The mechanic who checked the car reckoned the owner needed to spend £20,000 to put everything right and make it roadworthy. (Alternatively, the garage offered to pay £12,000 for the car – intending to break it and sell the parts.) The owner decided that instead of spending the £20,000, he would simply get the essentials sorted. And then, when he took the car out for a run, he discovered a leak. Investigation showed that the leak was coming from the heater and that it would cost £2,500 to put right because to deal with the leak, the front wing and the door would have to be removed. So the owner left the heater leaking. 'If you want to take the Rolls Royce out in the winter…wrap up warm. If you want to take it out in the summer, it's perfect.'

That is precisely our philosophy. Trying to repair everything would cost a fortune – so we're just repairing what has to be repaired.

My initial instruction to the garage was simple: look first at the brakes and then do everything that needs to be done to make the car safe and roadworthy.

The owner writing about his car in the magazine also reports that his car's radio (which is original) doesn't work. But he likes the look of it.

When I read this, I realised that we haven't yet tried our radio to see if it works. We enjoy our trips out without the radio and I suspect we'll continue that way. Maybe one day I'll try it to see if it works. Maybe that's a little surprise to come. The radio is also equipped with a cassette tape player and I have no idea when it was installed.

The undeniable fact is that a 67-year-old car isn't going to work quite as well as it did when it was new. But who am I to complain? My hearing is going, I can't read a book without spectacles, I feel knackered if I walk up hills, I have developing Dupuytren's contracture on both hands and I get a variety of unpleasant pains if I have to carry heavy bags of logs. I used to be able to do100 press ups on my fingertips but these days I'm glad there is a grab handle fixed above the bath. But none of that means that I am ready for the scrapheap any more than the fact that an old Bentley has a few niggles means that it cannot be driven and enjoyed. We use our new-old car regularly and it is an absolute delight.

Mickey Spillane is one of my heroes for one quip alone. Spillane wrote some of the most successful books of the 20th century – thrillers starring his hero Mike Hammer. He loved animals and described himself as a softie. He died in 2006 at the age of 88. The literary establishment found Spillane's unprecedented and unequalled success hard to swallow. 'Once,' Spillane recalled, 'some New York literary guy approached me at a party and said 'I think it's disgraceful that of the ten best-selling books of all time, seven were written by you.' Spillane replied: 'You're lucky that I've only written seven books'.'

I refuse to use electricity created by wind or solar farms since these are inefficient systems which are bad for the environment.

Part of the sun visor on the front passenger's side of the Bentley has fallen off. Looking at it I think I can repair it with a little glue. This will probably save us approximately £3,000 and six weeks without the car. When I do the repair I will check that the visor on the driver's side of the car isn't likely to fall off. I may spread a little glue around just to make sure.

I am fascinated by words. I have even written a dictionary of unusual Victorian words. It was fun to research and to compile. I re-discovered today that the word 'sultana' has, since the late 16th century, meant the wife or concubine of a sultan or, indeed, any woman in a sultan's family. The meaning of the word as a small, brown, seedless fruit made from green grapes and used in puddings and cakes is relatively modern and dates only from the mid 19th century. So, the primary meaning of the word 'sultana' is: 'a female member of a sultan's family'. And if you see a recipe which requires you to include sultanas then you are being invited to enter the world of cannibalism. Raisins, if you are interested, are made from any varieties of grapes and have no relevance in this excursion into the world of etymology.

I don't know whether this only happens to me but I receive a constant stream of requests to complete surveys and lengthy questionnaires. Companies and government departments are no longer satisfied with a quick 'like' or 'dislike'. Instead, I find myself being requested to fill in questionnaires that, they promise dishonestly, 'will take only three, five, seven minutes of your time'. And it's quite clear that the questions are designed not to discover whether I was happy with the service or item I have purchased but to collect as much personal information as possible. Many of the questions are quite intrusive. Today, for example, one of the four survey requests I received was from the National Health Service, which wanted me to work my way through a 53 question form ostensibly to find out my views on my GP and the service he or she provides. The questions included: 'What is your religion?' 'What is your ethnic group?' Is your gender identity the same as the sex you were registered at birth?' 'Which of the following best describes you: female, male non binary, prefer to self-describe, I would prefer not to say' and 'which of the following options best describes how you think of yourself? Heterosexual or straight, gay or lesbian, bisexual, other, I would prefer not to say'.

The form assures me that those who are collecting the forms 'will keep my answers completely confidential but there is an access code which will clearly tell them my identity, and anyone who trusts any official body to keep their answers confidential has obviously been living in a cave for a long time.

In the same post, I also received a questionnaire ostensibly sent by the Prime Minister. He wanted to know (among other things) how I voted at the last election.

The Bentley has been steaming up for a while. Whenever we used it, the windows are steamed up and the car feels damp when we open the doors. So I bought a large pack of desiccant sachets – the sort that are included in with electrical equipment –and when they came I distributed them around the car (in the door pockets and on the back window sill).

It's a miracle.

The car no longer steams up. And it does not feel damp.

I feel I have invented one of those useful tips which one reads about in magazines occasionally. There must be some periodical somewhere to which I can send this tip and win a £5 voucher for car cleaning products.

The car does have a system to remove condensation from the windscreen and there is a switch which can be turned on in order to deal with condensation on the back window. The switch, curiously, is on the back window shelf and tricky to reach for anyone other than a contortionist so I leave it in the 'on' position.

However, and whisper this quietly please, the windscreen demist system doesn't seem to work terribly well. I have no idea how well the system worked 67 years ago but today it is what we in the old cars world refer to as limited in efficiency.

I have no idea why this is but in my experience the demist facilities on old cars rarely work well at all. We could have sent the car into the garage for more investigations and more expensive restoration work. The car would have been away for weeks and the cost would have almost certainly run into thousands. But, instead, we decided to keep the car with us and to deal with the problem ourselves.

Putting a few handfuls of absorbent silica gel desiccant sachets into the car has made a huge difference. Car manufacturers could save thousands of pounds per car if they stopped installing complex and expensive demisting systems and merely gave each owner a supply of absorbent sachets.

On the rare occasions when the desiccant sachets don't work, we have another system for dealing with mist.

In the glove compartment or cubby hole on the driver's side of the car, I put a handful of old-fashioned yellow dusters (the ones with the red stitching around the edge). When the windscreen becomes misty, I simply wipe it with one of my dusters. Antoinette wipes her side of the windscreen. It takes but a moment and is, indeed, faster than any electrical demisting system on any modern car. Since the system is operated with the aid of our fingers I call it the Digital Demist Programme.

We were so pleased with our solution that we have bought twelve of the old-fashioned yellow dusters (the ones with red blanket stitching around the edge) at the very reasonable price of £3.85 for the dozen. The dusters are excellent in quality and much more efficient than paper tissues when used to wipe the inside of the windscreen.

And so we have replaced the car's own rather frail demisting system with a manually controlled demist facility which is quick and easy to use, very cheap and utterly reliable. However efficient your car's demist facility might be I bet we can demist our windscreen more speedily.

For decades now, we have been told that technology will improve our lives immeasurably. It is now clear that this was (and is) a lie.

Technology has given us electric car windows and CD players but it has done nothing to improve productivity, to improve health or, indeed, to improve life in any way. Technology has certainly done nothing to make people happier. On the contrary, technology invades our privacy, prevents us from repairing our own machinery and exposes us to ridicule, hacking and identity theft.

The big technology companies claim that they are doing 'good things' but it is clear that their sole aim is not to serve us but to extract data from us so that they can sell it to people who will use it to make our lives more complicated and more stressful.

For the big technology companies and the internet companies, we have become the product; the companies vie with one another to control us, to dominate our every waking (and sleeping) hour, to waste our time and to watch everything we do – so that they can sell our secrets to other companies for profit.

Something called Tik-Tok (which was popular with dancing nurses during the lockdowns, when hospitals were more or less shut and the staff had too little to do) enables China to monitor one billion users (including two thirds of all American teenagers). Tik-Tok's owner, a company called ByteDance is said to be obliged to share its data with the Chinese Communist Party. The Tik-Tok app traces users' locations and internet browsing activities. Moreover, the algorithm can be altered without informing users. Like YouTube and other censorious internet riff-raff, Tik-Tok has already censored users.

Amazingly, most people seem to find all this quite acceptable, even exciting.

And, of course, many internet consumers pay good money to have Amazon's scary Alexa device in their homes and don't seem to care that the damned thing can and does record their private conversations – and that real live humans can and do then listen to what they said.

The popularity of the companies producing technology can best be summarised by the fact that the value of Apple (the company that makes iPhones and iPads) is greater than the value of the entire UK stock market. And the value of the top seven technology companies in America (including Apple, Facebook and Google) is the same as the value of all the companies in Japan, Britain, China, France and Canada combined.

Now that I'm old I am, I think, officially allowed to look back at the world as it used to be and to pick out some of the things I miss. Here, off the top of my shrinking head, is a small list:

I miss old-fashioned tea shops (even ones spelt 'tea shoppe') where it was possible to buy a cream tea, a Welsh rarebit, a hot buttered crumpet or a toasted teacake and a decent cup of Earl Grey tea, served with a plateful of neat lemon slices. Devotion to the absurdities of the extremes of modern pseudoscience means that it will soon be impossible to find any eatery which sells anything more substantial than a slug and gnat salad. Maybe, in ten years' time, diners will protest vehemently if they find a small piece of lettuce leaf polluting their pure slug salad. Thanks to the European Union it is now nigh on impossible to obtain Lapsang Souchong tea at all. Apparently the bureaucrats have decided that it is too dangerous. I love good, old-fashioned cafes. I'm not sure why, but I do. The last time I was in Vienna there were still dozens of marvellous old cafes which have been serving their customers coffee and cakes since the days when people travelled around on horseback or in horse drawn conveyances. England in general, and London in particular, was the original home of the coffee house but today all we have left are the chain stores which sell mildly drinkable coffee in a plastic environment where the staff call themselves baristas but know nothing and care less . But there are occasional exceptions. The other day I discovered a local café which is run by a cheery Italian and his wife. They know what a café should do and what it should be to its customers. They are always cheery, they bring drinks to your table, they play opera music (quietly) in the background, they have a pile of newspapers for customers to read and they happily take cash.

If someone ever starts a campaign to bring back plastic bags, I will join the campaign instantly. We have our groceries delivered every week and the absence of plastic bags means that the whole process takes three times as long and is far more exhausting. The delivery van is parked outside the house for three times as long (usually with the engine burning diesel to keep the chilled compartment cold) and the costs for everyone are magnified. And the plastic bags were always either returned or used. The plastic bag was one of the most useful inventions of the 20th century and it required very little energy to make. (Paper bags and cotton bags require far more energy and water to make and distribute and are much worse for the environment.) The demise of the plastic bag is something to be mourned. People who dumped plastic bags in the wild needed to be punished but it made no sense to punish everyone by completely banning plastic bags.

Sport on terrestrial television is a real loss to the quality of life. Without live sports programmes, television is of no value whatsoever. There was, I seem to remember, a weekend in July when it was possible to watch the Open Golf Championship, the British Grand Prix, the Lord's Test Match and the final days of the Tour de France all on terrestrial television. I expect those events still go on but they go on without me. I miss them less these days but their disappearance has taken a little of the excitement out of life. Today, all we are left with is the tennis at Wimbledon. Is it a coincidence that the sports which have disappeared were all sports which appealed mainly to men and the sport which remains on terrestrial television is the sport which appeals mainly to women and BBC employees? It's perhaps not surprising that we never watch programmes on television and our television set is used to show videos (or, rather, DVDs).

In the olden days, a man (it was always a man) used to come round every few months to read the gas and electricity meters. These days we are expected to read our own meters. We have been co-opted as unpaid employees working as volunteers for the energy companies. And once the meters have been read, the results have to be emailed to the energy company. In our case, the whole process is infinitely more time consuming than it should be since the company which brought us our gas supply insisted on putting the gas meter 100 yards up our lane on the outside of our garage. If we don't send in our meter readings we get an estimated reading and an estimated bill which is invariably absurdly high so that we end up lending the energy company thousands of pounds we don't owe them.

The English Gentleman is as dead as the dodo. There are none in the House of Commons and definitely none in the House of Lords. There are none in the royal family or the aristocracy. It used to be possible to spot one or two at Lord's Cricket Ground but, sadly, those days are gone. The last gentlemen were those who appeared in fiction: John Buchan's great hero Richard Hannay and the protagonists from Buchan's real masterpiece 'John McNab'; Sapper's Hugh 'Bulldog' Drummond (the prototype for James Bond); Dorothy L. Sayers' aristocratic detective Lord Peter Wimsey; Dornford Yates's great creations, Bertram 'Berry' Pleydell and Jonathan Mansel; Francis Durbridge's Paul Temple; Dashiel Hammet's Thin Man (Nick Charles – given flesh and blood by William Powell in the largely forgotten but evergreen series of films in which he starred with Myrna Loy) and, of course, Bertie Wooster, a chevalier of the drawing room. James Bond, now gone of course, was never a gentleman and if reinvented will be merely a pastiche of a pastiche. I'm delighted to report that of this elite list of gentlemen, the immortal Bulldog Drummond is reportedly the favourite male literary 'pin-up' of the staff of the BBC and The Guardian newspaper.

I miss seeing 'Kilroy was here' scrawled in strange places. On a visit to East Berlin in the 1970s, I managed to leave numerous 'Kilroy was here' messages (scrawled in white chalk, as they should be). And when Stalin attended the Potsdam Conference, he found those famous three words scrawled on a loo wall. But Kilroy seems to have been deleted from public life. I miss him. And, curiously, I also miss the work of those artists who used to draw moustaches and spectacles onto posters. Back in 1966, PG Wodehouse reported, apparently with some regret, that the Transit Authority in the US was fining people $250 for pencilling moustaches onto the faces on posters in the subway.

Cassette tapes (both the audio variety and the type used for watching films) were much better than CDs and DVDs. You could stop a cassette tape or DVD half way through and then go back to the exact spot a week later. When CDs and DVDs were introduced, we were promised that they would never fail or go wrong. In practice, they are no more reliable than cassettes and with a cassette you could always mend most problems by using a pencil to wind the tape a little tighter. Moreover, I also miss our old video recorder. I could use it to record films I wanted to watch at a more convenient time. Occasionally, I set it to record television programmes I'd made so that I could spin through and see what a mess I'd made of things. We now have a DVD player which seems unwilling to play DVDs and, as far as I am able to make out, is quite incapable of recording them. How anyone can call a DVD player better than a video recorder is quite beyond me.

I miss decent road signs. In the old days, road signs would carry distances in miles. Today there are no distances marked. I assume that the distances are omitted because the authorities are waiting to get rid of Imperial measurements, expecting that in future distances will have to be measured in kilometres. And, of course, most cars these days are fitted with satellite navigation systems. (The Bentley was built many decades before satellite navigation was available but it does have a cigar lighter. And if we want a satellite navigation system, we can simply fit a portable one into the cigar lighter. Actually, there are, as you might expect, two cigar lighters in the car – one for the driver and the front passenger, and one in the rear of the car, for the passengers in the rear. You didn't think there would only be one, did you?)

I miss cricket very much. When I was a boy I loved cricket, and when I was a GP I used to spend my half day off watching cricket. Back then cricket was worth watching. Modern cricketers think they invented cricket as entertainment but in 1900, at Lords cricket ground, GL Jessop (a great amateur cricketer) scored 157 runs out of 201 in 60 minutes playing for Gloucestershire against the West Indies. This was by no means exceptional for Jessop. Modern cricketers who fancy themselves as entertainers should remember that Jessop was playing with far less adequate equipment on a pitch that modern grounds-men would regard as too rough to be used as the outfield. Worst of all, cricket has become painfully woke and politically correct. The England and Wales Cricket Board is pouring £100 million into women's domestic cricket. Not surprisingly, they forecast a loss of £86.7 million over five seasons.

I miss junk shops and dusty, second-hand book shops very much. I'm quick to admit that the internet is wonderful for finding books when I know what I'm looking for. But there is no doubt that those serendipitous, chance discoveries are rarer. There are still one or two junk shops available (though the owner invariably calls them something grander than 'junk shops'). Browsing among a few shelves of battered old paperbacks, I found a copy of a book called 'Mrs Harris goes to Moscow' by Paul Gallico and a copy of an autobiographical volume by Donald Swann entitled (curiously) 'The Space between the Bars'. I would never have found either of these books on the internet because I didn't know they existed. I thought Paul Gallico's wonderful series about Mrs Harris had ended with her becoming an MP and I didn't know that Donald Swann (the piano playing half of Flanders and Swann, the duo who entertained and captivated theatre audiences and LP record buyers in the years after the Second World War, with shows such as 'At the Drop of a Hat') had written any books. When the last junk shop closes and the last book shop shuts its doors, and we are left with online eBay sellers running their businesses from spare bedrooms and lock up garages, there will be no serendipitous discoveries and life will become much poorer for it. It is true, by the way, that there are a few antique markets around where a number of dealers take space within a small mall. However, all the stalls are run by professional specialists and everything is always overpriced and bargains are non-existent. If you're looking for a specific item they're great but if you're a browser and impulse buyer these stalls are usually disappointing. I miss junk shops which sold anything and everything – where the owner measured his stock by quantity rather than quality. Hidden among the dross you could often find gold.

The absurd enthusiasm for 20 mph limits has nothing whatsoever to do with road safety, of course, but is triggered by a desire to stop any sort of travel, especially motorised travel which provides motorists with independence. There are apparently 692 campaign groups campaigning for 20 mph limits in Britain alone, and one assumes that they don't realise that the 20 mph limits have been shown to increase the likelihood of accidents, increase the amount of fuel used, increase the amount of pollution, increase the length of journeys, increase the risk of breakdowns, dramatically reduce productivity and increase response times for ambulances and fire engines (the drivers of which are not, unlike the police, allowed to exceed speed limits. It is often alleged that cars use less fuel at 20 mph. This is a blatant lie. None of our three cars uses less fuel when going slowly. High performance cars such as our Maserati are most efficient when travelling at between 70 mph and 80 mph – though naturally I would never dream of travelling at such a speed on public roads. And when fuel consumption goes up, so does the amount of pollution. A recent study showed that at 20 mph, the amount of air pollution is 35% higher than it is when travelling at 30 mph.

Town and city driving at 20 mph is a miserable, dangerous and exhausting business but travelling outside built up areas isn't much more fun either. Politicians in Wales introduced 20 mph limits on well over a third of that country's roads and then had to change the speed limits back to a more sensible figure because of the vast number of complaints which resulted. What a pity they didn't do a trial before introducing blanket 20 mph limits that were never going to be acceptable.

Road works which remain in situ so long that they really need planning permission, and absurd speed limits, which change every few hundred yards and which are policed by an endless variety of cameras aided and abetted by insane citizens armed with their own speed cameras and mobile phones, endless queues of lorries (now that there are no reliable railway services, companies have had to go back to moving stuff around the country by road) and far too many cars mean that travel, especially on motorways, is a slow and tedious business. When I was a boy, my parents had a Morris which would, if travelling downhill with the wind behind it, hit 60 mph. And yet when going on holiday to Cornwall, or just travelling around for days out, we routinely expected to average over 40 mph. I suspect that it is a long time since any driver in Britain has travelled for an hour in the daytime and covered 40 miles.

People up to around the 1960s were infinitely more thrifty than people are today. My parents used to save anything and everything. Christmas wrapping paper had to be removed carefully, smoothed out and kept for another Christmas. My father kept every small screw and odd bits of wood – and used them. And my mother saved paper bags, buttons and bits of string. She wasn't alone. A woman who was a patient of mine (and who, for reasons which I never quite understand, always explained away every curious event by commenting 'Well, it was a leap year') reported that when she cleared out her father's desk she had found a used envelope with the words 'Bits of string too short for use' written neatly on the side that had not been used for the address.

The Bentley struggles a little to get up steep hills. No, that's not fair. It doesn't struggle, so much as think about things fairly deeply when asked to tackle a steep hill. When it is apparent that the hill is becoming steeper, the car slows, pauses, ponders, calibrates and talks to itself for a while, looks around, assesses the slope ahead and then, and only then, moves into a lower gear before continuing.

I'm not complaining. I'm much the same myself.

I totter around these days and stop and look at the countryside more than I used to do. Indeed, I'm thinking of digging out my old 35 mm pocket camera and carrying it with me. When I find myself struggling to get up a hill, I'll take out the camera and look through the viewfinder as though contemplating taking a photograph. This will enable me to stop and take what is, I believe, known as a 'breather' whenever I find myself running low on puff or muscle power.

Like most people over the age of 15, I have learned that avoiding unnecessary risks is generally wise. I don't jump out of aeroplanes (with or without a parachute) and I wouldn't dream of taking up bungee jumping. Both are extraordinarily dangerous activities which, incidentally, result in so many serious injuries that they cost the health services huge amounts of money. Taking care when crossing the road makes sense, steering well clear of noisy dogs is merely rational and keeping well out of the way of people who are constantly coughing is a sensible precaution.

But many people seem to feel that we all need to be protected from every possible risk, whatever the cost might be to everyone else.

So, the growing number of people who claim (rightly or wrongly) that they or their children suffer from nut allergies and insist that restaurants should stop serving anything containing nuts, that manufacturers and retailers must label their packaging with absurd notices about nuts, and that children in nurseries and infant schools should have anything which might (just might) contain nuts removed from their luncheon boxes (presumably in case a fellow pupil should steal some item of food which might do them harm) are making life miserable for everyone.

The absurd business of protecting people from every possible danger now means that one of the best and most effective forms of anaesthesia is allegedly banned because one or two people might harm themselves by using it recreationally, and the best medicine for a persistent cough (codeine linctus) has been banned from over the counter sale in case people take it and become addicted. Worse still, doctors are so frightened of patients becoming addicted to painkillers, that they refuse to prescribe adequate pain relief even when it is clearly necessary.

The odd thing is that this bizarre and unscientific obsession with risk, and with staying healthy at all costs, means that most of the population in all so-called developed countries now take daily medication of one sort or another to keep them healthy, ignoring the fact that most of the medication is unnecessary and likely to cause uncomfortable, dangerous or deadly side effects.

When it was first opened, women were not allowed to set foot on the Forth Bridge in case a gust of wind blew them over the edge. The assumption was that voluminous skirts would make life too dangerous for them.

We all tend to forget stuff but as we get older we (and those around us) begin to worry when we forget things. We worry, inevitably, that we may be showing early signs of dementia or, more specifically, of Alzheimer's disease – the most over-diagnosed disease in the world at the moment. It is the default diagnosis for anyone who is regarded by their relatives or their doctor as being forgetful.

My wife will know I have lost all my senses if I:
Say something complimentary about a politician
Ask for tripe or brains for supper

Say I'm not hungry
Announce that I think I'll catch up on my missed vaccinations
Carry a comb upon my person
Jump up excitedly when I hear the telephone ring
Set the alarm clock for 6 am so I can get a good start on the day
Start watching television
Pay the TV licence fee in order to give money to the BBC
Buy an electric car (other than one I can put battcrics in and race about the garden)

We sat in the Bentley in a traffic queue today and after a few minutes I began to feel edgy. There was no reason for this. We weren't in a hurry. We didn't have to be anywhere in a rush. And then I realised why I felt uncomfortable. Our Maserati doesn't like queues. The salesman who sold us the car warned us to keep out of queues as much as possible. The car has a high performance Ferrari engine and it gets terribly upset if it has to trundle along at 10 mph or sit quietly and do nothing. Unless it is parked, it really needs to travel at 40 mph or more in order to feel comfortable. If we ever go to Wales we'll need to travel in something else.

But the Bentley doesn't mind waiting at all. It just sits and purrs and waits. And sits and purrs and waits.

If there is a keynote word for the 21st century in Britain it is 'waiting'. We all wait for everything. And the waiting is interminable. We wait for trains and buses and aeroplanes which are usually late and often cancelled and so never arrive. We wait for security to search our bags and our clothing. We wait for an appointment to see a doctor and we wait for hospital appointments and when we arrive (on time) we are kept waiting for hours. We wait for test results – living on tenterhooks for weeks and sometimes months as we wait to be reassured or to know the worst. We wait for replies when we contact banks, utilities or public services. We wait for hours if we try to telephone the tax people.

The people of Britain wait more and longer than the people of any other country. And the people who keep us waiting do not seem to care. Maybe they do not care because they know that when it is their turn to need something they too will be kept waiting. Maybe they keep people waiting as a sort of sick revenge. Waiting is the new British disease. It is not surprising that productivity is appalling and worse in Britain than anywhere else in the world.

Driving used to be fun.

Crowded roads, uncertain speed limits, a plethora of useless and misleading road signs (and an absence of useful mileage indicators) have combined with speed cameras and irrational speed limits to take away the fun. New regulations and bizarre laws which force motorists to give cyclists so much space that overtaking on many roads is quite impossible, have deliberately made driving a nightmare.

Driving in a 1957 Bentley takes us back to better times. The world outside seems quite different when you're bowling along in an old car without all the driving aids which are now considered essential. The car is so big that it's like piloting a great liner on the open seas. Drivers of racing cars are called pilots and drivers of old Bentleys should be called captains.

And once again the getting there is just as important, and just as much a part of the journey, as the arriving or the being there.

Today, we sometimes just go for a drive for the fun of it. We never do that in the Maserati. How long since you went for a drive just for fun?

We have found that the answer to all the organised misery known as 'foreign travel' is to stay at home with a pile of good books to read, a selection of good DVDs to watch and a pantry full of our favourite foods. When we want to take a break we turn off the telephone, the doorbell and any devices which connect to the outside world. We don't much like visitors, especially the uninvited variety, and don't respond to the doorbell if it rings unexpectedly.

When I was very young we used to visit a Great Aunt occasionally. She was well into her eighties and lived in an Alms House which she never left. She had a budgie and always fed us caraway seed cake which now I think of it was probably made with the seeds the budgie hadn't eaten. Visits had to be announced at least a fortnight in advance. And since she had no telephone this meant an exchange of letters. At the time I never understood why she needed so much notice of an intended visit. Now I do.

Staying at home means we don't have to worry about strikes, hold ups, customs officers, lost luggage or any of the other commonplace annoyances which drive travellers mad. We don't have to give our fingerprints either. (All travellers are now officially regarded as ipso facto default criminals.) And nor do we have to worry about parcels being left on the doorstep while we are away, about burglars popping round to steal our collection of kindling or about whether we remembered to turn off the gas.

When we go out we rarely travel more than 10 miles away from home. An adventure is to travel 30 miles away from home. In the 21st century, home sweet home is the place to be.

I used to think I would find it difficult never to see Paris again. We had an apartment there for 20 years. But I now know that I can live without seeing it again. The city's politicians have made the city unfriendly and unwelcoming. We have plenty of photos and postcards if our memories fail us.

The writer G.K.Chesterton (who was the author of, among other things, the Father Brown stories) was at home in Battersea, London and was packing in preparation for a holiday when a friend called round. 'Where are you going?' inquired the friend. 'To Battersea,' replied Chesterton. When the friend expressed bewilderment, Chesterton explained that he was going abroad for a while so that he could come back home and once again discover its joys and beauties. His short-term destination could have been anywhere; his long-term destination was simply 'home'. He wanted to go away so that he could come back.

The Bentley is still smooth and powerful, and I am now entirely comfortable when it struggles a little when climbing steep hills. The automatic gearbox thinks for a second or two before changing down. I sympathise. I used to be able to do a hundred different things in a day. When I was working as a GP I still managed to race around on my time off to make TV and radio programmes. And at nights and weekends I used the free time between calls to write books, five weekly columns and two monthly columns as well as running various campaigns. Today, I feel exhausted after I've spent two hours working on a book. I understand our old Bentley and don't laugh but I think it understands me. We have what used to be called a rapport.

I am puzzled and saddened by the fact that the things I used to regard as good, and the people I admired and respected, are now sneered at and derided.

Honour, respect, dignity and honesty are dismissed as old-fashioned and irrelevant. Patriotism is now a heinous sin. We are all supposed to be world citizens, directed by billionaires who have different values to the rest of us.

It used to be possible to tell the good guys from the bad guys. These days, it's difficult.

But the Bentley, faded glory but still solid and reliable, is a constant reminder of another time. It sits outside waiting to do what it was built to do.

May you have peace and smiles each day and may you be constantly surprised and occasionally overwhelmed by considered and deliberate kindnesses.

Appendix 1
Author Biography

Sunday Times bestselling author Vernon Coleman qualified as a doctor in 1970 and has worked both in hospitals and as a principal in general practice. Vernon Coleman is a multi-million selling author. He has written over 100 books which have sold over three million copies in the UK, been in bestseller lists around the world and been translated into 26 languages. Several of his books have been on the bestseller lists and in the UK, paperback editions of his books have been published by Pan, Penguin, Corgi, Arrow, Century, RKP, Mandarin and Star among many others. His novel 'Mrs Caldicot's Cabbage War' was turned into a successful, award winning movie and his play of the same name has been produced by amateur drama societies. He has presented numerous programmes on television and radio, including several series based on his best-selling book Bodypower which was voted one of the 100 most popular books by British readers.

Vernon Coleman has written columns for the Daily Star, Sun, Sunday Express, Planet on Sunday and The People and has contributed over 5,000 articles, columns and reviews to 100 leading British publications including Daily Telegraph, Sunday Telegraph, Guardian, Observer, Sunday Times, Daily Mail, Mail on Sunday, Daily Express, Woman, Woman's Own, Punch and Spectator. His columns and articles have also appeared in hundreds of leading magazines and newspapers throughout the rest of the world. His travel articles were illustrated with his own photographs and his cartoons have appeared in many magazines. He edited the British Clinical Journal and founded and edited the European Medical Journal. For twenty years he wrote a column which was syndicated to over 40 leading regional newspapers in the UK and to papers all around the world. He was a Professor of Holistic Medical Science and has lectured at three medical schools.

In the UK, Vernon Coleman was the TV AM doctor on breakfast TV and the first networked television Agony Aunt, working on the BBC. Many millions consulted his Telephone Doctor advice lines, and for six years he wrote a monthly newsletter which had subscribers in 17 countries.

Since the early 1990s he has had a website (www.vernoncoleman.com) and the latest figures show that between 25 and 30 million people read his web articles each month.

Vernon Coleman has a medical degree, and an honorary science doctorate. He has worked for the Open University in the UK and was an honorary Professor of Holistic Medical Sciences at the Open International University based in Sri Lanka. He worked as a general practitioner for ten years (resigning from the NHS after being fined for refusing to divulge confidential information about his patients to State bureaucrats) and has organised numerous campaigns both for people and for animals. He has given evidence to both the House of Commons and the House of Lords in the UK. He can ride a bicycle and swim, though not at the same time. He likes animals, cafés and collecting cigarette cards. Vernon Coleman is a bibliophile and has a library larger than most towns. He used to enjoy cricket when it was played as a sport by gentlemen but lost heart when the authorities started painting advertisements on the grass. He loves log fires and making bonfires.

Since 1999 he has been very happily married to the professional artist and author, Donna Antoinette Coleman to whom he is devoted and with whom he has co-written five books. They live in the delightful if isolated village of Bilbury in Devon where they have designed for themselves a unique world to sustain and nourish them in these dark and difficult times. They rarely leave home though when they do it is usually in a 1957 Bentley.

For more information please visit: www.vernoncoleman.com or see his author page on Amazon.

Appendix 2
What the papers say:

'Vernon Coleman writes as a general practitioner who has become disquieted by the all-pervasive influence of the pharmaceutical industry in modern medicine…He describes, with a wealth of illustrations, the phenomena of modern iatrogenesis; but he is also concerned about the wider harm which can result from doctors' and patients' preoccupation with medication instead of with the prevention of disease. He demonstrates, all the more effectively because he writes in a sober, matter-of-fact style, the immense influence exercised by the drug industry on doctors' prescribing habits…He writes as a family doctor who is keenly aware of the social dimensions of medical practice. He ends his book with practical suggestions as to how medical care – in the developing countries as well as in the West – can best be freed from this unhealthy pharmaceutical predominance.' – G.M.Carstairs, The Times Literary Supplement (1975)

'What he says of the present is true: and it is the great merit of the book that he says it from the viewpoint of a practising general practitioner, who sees from the inside what is going on, and is appalled by the consequences to the profession, and to the public.' – Brian Inglis, Punch (1975)

'Dr Coleman writes with more sense than bias. Required reading for any Minister of Health' – Daily Express

'I hope this book becomes a bestseller among doctors, nurses and the wider public…' – Nursing Times

'Dr Coleman's well-coordinated book could not be more timely.' – Yorkshire Post

'Few would disagree with Dr Coleman that more should be done about prevention.' – The Lancet

'This short but very readable book has a message that is timely. Vernon Coleman's point is that much of the medical research into which money and expertise are poured is useless. At the same time, remedial conditions of mind and body which cause the most distress are largely neglected. This is true.' – Daily Telegraph

'If you believe Dr Vernon Coleman, the main beneficiaries of the hundred million pounds worth of research done in this country each year are certainly not the patients. The research benefits mostly the medical place seekers, who use their academic investigations as rungs on the promotional ladder, or drug companies with an eye for the latest market opening…The future may hold bionic superman but all a nation's physic cannot significantly change the basic mortality statistics except sometimes, to make them worse.' – The Guardian

'Dr Coleman's well-coordinated book could not be more timely.' – Yorkshire Post

'The Medicine Men is well worth reading' – Times Educational Supplement

'Dr Vernon Coleman…is not a mine of information – he is a fountain. It pours out of him, mixed with opinions which have an attractive common sense ring about them.' – Coventry Evening Telegraph

'When the children have finished playing the games on your Sinclair or Commodore Vic 20 computer, you can turn it to more practical purposes. For what is probably Britain's first home doctor programme for computers is now available. Dr Vernon Coleman, one of the country's leading medical authors, has prepared the text for a remarkable series of six cassettes called The Home Doctor Series. Dr Coleman, author of the new book 'Bodypower'…has turned his attention to computers.' – The Times 1983

'The Medicine Men' by Dr Vernon Coleman, was the subject of a 14 minute 'commercial' on the BBC's Nationwide television programme recently. Industry doctors and general practitioners come in for a severe drubbing: two down and several more to go because the targets for Dr Coleman's pen are many, varied and, to say the least, surprising. Take the physicians who carry out clinical trials: many of those, claims the author, have sold themselves to the industry and agreed to do research for rewards of one kind or another, whether that reward be a trip abroad, a piece of equipment, a few dinners, a series of published papers or simply money.' – The Pharmaceutical Journal

'By the year 2020 there will be a holocaust, not caused by a plutonium plume but by greed, medical ambition and political opportunism. This is the latest vision of Vernon Coleman, an articulate and prolific medical author…this disturbing book detects diseases in the whole way we deliver health care.' – Sunday Times (1988)

'…the issues explores he explores are central to the health of the nation.' – Nursing Times

'It is not necessary to accept his conclusion to be able to savour his decidedly trenchant comments on today's medicine…a book to stimulate and to make one argue.' – British Medical Journal

'As a writer of medical bestsellers, Dr Vernon Coleman's aim is to shock us out of our complacency…it's impossible not to be impressed by some of his arguments.' – Western Daily Press

'Controversial and devastating' – Publishing News

'Dr Coleman produces mountains of evidence to justify his outrageous claims.' – Edinburgh Evening News

'Dr Coleman lays about him with an uncompromising verbal scalpel, dipped in vitriol, against all sorts of sacred medical cows.' – Exeter Express and Echo

'Vernon Coleman writes brilliant books.' – The Good Book Guide

'No thinking person can ignore him. This is why he has been for over 20 years one of the world's leading advocates on human and animal rights in relation to health. Long may it continue.' – The Ecologist

'The calmest voice of reason comes from Dr Vernon Coleman.' – The Observer

'A godsend.' – Daily Telegraph

'Dr Vernon Coleman has justifiably acquired a reputation for being controversial, iconoclastic and influential.' – General Practitioner

'Superstar.' – Independent on Sunday

'Brilliant!' – The People

'Compulsive reading.' – The Guardian

'His message is important.' – The Economist

'He's the Lone Ranger, Robin Hood and the Equalizer rolled into one.' – Glasgow Evening Times

'The man is a national treasure.' – What Doctors Don't Tell You

'His advice is optimistic and enthusiastic.' – British Medical Journal

'Revered guru of medicine.' – Nursing Times

'Gentle, kind and caring' – Western Daily Press

'His trademark is that he doesn't mince words. Far funnier than the usual tone of soupy piety you get from his colleagues.' – The Guardian

'Dr Coleman is one of our most enlightened, trenchant and sensitive dispensers of medical advice.' – The Observer

'Vernon Coleman is a leading medical authority and known to

millions through his writing, broadcasting and bestselling books.' – Woman's Own

'His book Bodypower is one of the most sensible treatises on personal survival that has ever been published.' – Yorkshire Evening Post

'One of the country's top health experts.' – Woman's Journal

'Dr Coleman is crusading for a more complete awareness of what is good and bad for our bodies. In the course of that he has made many friends and some powerful enemies.' – Western Morning News

'Brilliant.' – The People

'Dr Vernon Coleman is one of our most enlightened, trenchant and sensible dispensers of medical advice.' – The Observer

'The most influential medical writer in Britain. There can be little doubt that Vernon Coleman is the people's doctor.' – Devon Life

'The medical expert you can't ignore.' – Sunday Independent

'A literary genius.' – HSL Newsletter

'I would much rather spend an evening in his company than be trapped for five minutes in a radio commentary box with Mr Geoffrey Boycott.' – Peter Tinniswood, Punch

'Hard hitting...inimitably forthright.' – Hull Daily Mail

'Refreshingly forthright.' – Liverpool Daily Post

'Outspoken and alert.' – Sunday Express

'The man with a mission.' – Morning News

'A good read...very funny and packed with interesting and useful advice.' – The Big Issue

'Dr Coleman gains in stature with successive books' – Coventry Evening Telegraph

'Dr Coleman made me think again.' – BBC World Service

'Marvellously succinct, refreshingly sensible.' – The Spectator

'The living terror of the British medical establishment. A doctor of science as well as a medical graduate. Dr Coleman is probably one of the most brilliant men alive today. His extensive medical knowledge renders him fearless.' – Irish Times

'His future as King of the media docs is assured.' – The Independent

'Britain's leading medical author.' – The Star

'His advice is practical and readable.' – Northern Echo

'The layman's champion.' –Evening Herald

'All commonsense and no nonsense.' – Health Services Management

'One of Britain's leading experts.' – Slimmer Magazine

'The only three things I always read before the programme are Andrew Rawnsley in the Observer, Peter Hitchens in the Mail and Dr Vernon Coleman in The People. Or, if I'm really up against it, just Vernon Coleman.' – Eddie Mair, Presenter on BBC's Radio Four

'Dr Coleman is more illuminating than the proverbial lady with the lamp' – Company Magazine

'Britain's leading health care campaigner.' – The Sun

'What he says is true.' – Punch

'Perhaps the best known health writer for the general public in the world today.' – The Therapist

'The patient's champion. The doctor with the common touch.' – Birmingham Post

'A persuasive writer whose arguments, bascd on rcscarch and experience, are sound.' – Nursing Standard

'Coleman is controversial but respected and has been described in the British press as `the sharpest mind in medial journalism' and `the calmest voice of reason'. – Animals Today

'Vernon Coleman…rebel with a cause.' – Belfast Newsletter

'…presents the arguments against drug based medicine so well, and disturbs a harmful complacency so entertainingly.' – Alternative News

'He is certainly someone whose views are impossible to ignore, with his passionate advocacy of human and animal rights.' – International Journal of Alternative and Complementary Medicine

'The doctor who dares to speak his mind.' – Oxford Mail

'Dr Coleman speaks openly and reassuringly.' – Oxford Times

'He writes lucidly and wittily.' – Good Housekeeping

Printed in Great Britain
by Amazon

9266dd03-8529-4b79-8f66-6503bb54b58cR01